Plays of America
from American Folklore
for Children

Smith and Kraus *Books For Actors*
YOUNG ACTORS SERIES

Great Scenes and Monologues for Children
Great Scenes for Young Actors from the Stage
Great Monologues for Young Actors
Multicultural Monologues for Young Actors
Multicultural Scenes for Young Actors
Monologues from Classic Plays 468 BC to 1960 AD
Scenes from Classic Plays 468 BC to 1970 AD
New Plays from A.C.T.'s Young Conservatory Vol. I
New Plays from A.C.T.'s Young Conservatory Vol. II
Plays of America from American Folklore for Young Actors 7-12
Seattle Children's Theatre: Six Plays for Young Actors
Short Plays for Young Actors
Villeggiature: A Trilogy by Carlo Goldoni, *condenced for Young Actors*
Loving to Audition: The Audition Workbook for Young Actors
Movement Stories for Children
An Index of Plays for Young Actors
Discovering Shakespeare: **A Midsummer Night's Dream**,
    a workbook for students
Discovering Shakespeare: **Romeo and Juliet**, *a workbook*
    for students
Discovering Shakespeare: **The Taming of the Shrew,**
    a workbook for students

CAREER DEVELOPMENT SERIES

The Job Book: 100 Acting Jobs for Actors
The Job Book II: 100 Day Jobs for Actors
The Smith and Kraus Monologue Index
The Great Acting Teachers and Their Methods
The Actor's Guide to Qualified Acting Coaches: New York
The Actor's Guide to Qualified Acting Coaches: Los Angeles
The Camera Smart Actor
The Sanford Meisner Approach
Cold Readings: Some Do's and Don'ts for Actors at Auditions

If you require pre-publication information about upcoming Smith and Kraus books, you may receive our semi-annual catalogue, free of charge, by sending your name and address to *Smith and Kraus Catalogue, P.O. Box 127, One Main Street, Lyme, NH 03768. Or call us at (800) 895-4331, fax (603) 795-4427.*

Plays of America
from American Folklore
for Children

by L.E. McCullough

Young Actors Series

SK
A Smith and Kraus Book

A Smith and Kraus Book
Published by Smith and Kraus, Inc.
One Main Street, PO Box 127, Lyme, NH 03768

Copyright © 1996 by L.E. McCullough
All rights reserved
Manufactured in the United States of America
Cover and Text Design by Julia Hill

First Edition: March 1996
10 9 8 7 6 5 4 3 2 1

Library of Congress Cataloging-in-Publication Date

McCullough, L.E.
Plays of America from American folklore for children / by L.E. McCullough
p. cm. -- (Young actors series)
Summary: Fifteen original plays with themes taken from American folklore.
ISBN 1-57525-038-1
1. Folklore--United States--Juvenile drama. 2. Children's plays, American.
[1. Folklore--United States--Drama. 2. Plays.] I. Title. II. Series: Young actor series.
PS3563.C35297P58 1996
812'.54--dc20 96-1702
CIP
AC

Acknowledgements

The author wishes to thank the following for professional literary development and scholastic support:

Dr. Frances Rhome of Indiana University-Purdue University at Indianapolis; James Powell of the Writers' Center of Indianapolis; Tom and Yvonne Phelan of Pharaoh Audiobooks; Sean O'Sullivan of University College Dublin; Hugh Shields of Trinity College Dublin; Lee Gutkind of the University of Pittsburgh; Nancy Bogen of Twickenham Press; Nancy Kline, Director of the Writing Program at Barnard College; Robert Graham Small, Kathleen Tosco, Paul Hildebrand and the entire company of the 1995 Shenandoah International Playwrights Retreat—and—my wife, Kitty.

Dedication

Though I first came to formally study folklore at the Folklore Institute at Indiana University-Bloomington as a college undergraduate, my earliest interest in folktales came from my family—particularly two aunts, Catherine and Margaret Igoe, who during vacation outings at the New Jersey shore regaled me and my cousins with hilarious, terrifying ghost stories—and my parents, Isabel and Ervin McCullough, who on my fourth birthday made me a present of *My Book House,* an incredible series of story books edited by Olive Beaupré Miller that contained hundreds of folktales from around the globe, tales that inflamed my youthful imagination with an appetite for fancy and fantasy that has never abated. To them, and to all the other families throughout history who have passed down folklore to the next generation, I respectfully dedicate this book.

CONTENTS

Acknowledgements   v
Dedication vi
Foreword ix

K-3
How the People Got Fire   1
Let's Have a Hoedown! 11
The Cobbler's Pipe 27
Mr. & Mrs. Charlie T. Mule 37
Gluscabi and His Magic Game Bag 45
The Beggar in the Blanket 55
Patches Solves a Wedding Riddle 65
Magnus Fourpenny and the Black Bear Birthday Bash 73
The Laziest Girl in the World 83
Tillie Edelpickel's Sack of Lies 95

4-6
The Glass Mountain 105
The Honest Miller (El Molinero Honesto) 117
Shlemazl Goes to Paradise 129
The Most Expensive Bonnet in All Indiana 139
Return of the Red Phantom 151

FOREWORD

It's always seemed to me that legends and yarns and folktales are as much a part of the real history of a country as proclamations and provisos and constitutional amendments. The legends and the yarns get down to the roots of the people — they tell a good deal about what people admire and want, about what sort of people they are.

—Stephen Vincent Benét (1898-1943)
American poet and short-story writer

I'm the yaller blossom o' the forest! I'm half horse, half alligator and a mite touched with snappin' turtle! I can lick my weight in wildcats, hug a b'ar too close for comfort and wade the Mississippi! I'm a ring-tailed roarer, and I can out-dance any critter on land or sea or sky! Now, let's get on with this frolic, for I'm just gettin' warmed up, and I'm rarin' to go!

—Davy Crockett (1786-1836)
American congressman, soldier and folk legend

•

The fifteen plays in this book are drawn from the seemingly bottomless, ever-evolving fount of American folklore. They range from ancient Native American creation myths to European, African and Asian folktales recast in New World settings to popular retellings of actual incidents in United States history. Put them all in a pot, stir with a generous portion of salt and spice and you've got a succinct, savory sample of America's folk heritage ready for instant staging!

Many people today mistakenly believe that "folklore" is nothing more than weird stories about make-believe people in bygone days—fairy tales, Jack and the Beanstalk, Mother Goose, haunted houses and so forth. In fact, folklore has for centuries served as a major source of inspiration for some of the greatest musical, literary, dramatic and artistic works ever created, from symphonies, ballets and Broadway plays to movies, paintings and Pulitzer Prize-winning novels. Even as you read this sentence, folklore based on our own contemporary world is taking shape, coloring our perception of what we experience in the present and how we will be perceived by future generations looking to the past.

Folklore has always fulfilled an important educational function in human society, from earliest times to the present. Folklore transmits information about how the world came to be, providing concrete answers to the infinite variations of the question relentlessly posed to adults by children everywhere: "Why?" Folklore describes the group's accepted behavior standards—and what might happen if these standards are violated (taboo). Folklore communicates crucial knowledge about work, family rearing, warfare, worship and recreation. Far from being a collection of cultural leftovers or silly nursery stories, folklore is a distilled, superbly expressive synopsis of a group's shared history, social order and moral belief system.

Despite the fanciful nature of many of these plays, each is rooted in a historical or cultural reality that tells us much about the people who created it. Though the plays encompass a wide span of ethnic groups, time periods and geographic locales, each ultimately is concerned with some virtue or failing common to all humanity—cleverness and bravery in the face of danger, the foiling of vanity and greed, loyalty to family and friends, respect for the world we must all inhabit. While these works should not be viewed as "morality plays," they can serve as starting points for discussion about ethical issues of interest to children.

The *Plays of America* series has been designed to combine with studies in other disciplines: history, costume, language, dance, music, social studies, etc. If you are a music teacher and want to add some more sea shanties to *Return of the Red Phantom,* go ahead and make it a class project. *Gluscabi and His Magic Game Bag* can supplement lesson plans in environmental awareness and preservation. If your class is doing *The Honest Miller* in conjunction with an area study of the southwestern United States, feel free to have the characters speak a few additional lines of Spanish and decorate the set with southwestern architecture and plants. Each play has enough real-life historical and cultural references to support a host of pre- or post-play activities that integrate easily with related curriculum areas.

Besides those children enrolled in the onstage cast, others can be included in the production as lighting and sound technicians, prop masters, script coaches and stage managers. *Plays of America for Children* is an excellent vehicle for getting other members of the school and community involved in your project. Maybe there is an accomplished performer of Irish music in your area; ask them to play a few jigs and reels for *The Laziest Girl in the World.* Perhaps someone at your local historical society or library can give a talk about early American Christmas customs for *The Cobbler's Pipe;* a geology professor could add details about 19th-century mining operations for *The Glass Mountain.* Try utilizing the talents of local school or youth orchestra members to play incidental music...get the school art club to paint scrims and backdrops...see if a senior citizens' group might volunteer time to sew costumes...inquire whether an Asian restaurant might bring samples of Vietnamese cuisine for *The Beggar in the Blanket.*

Most of all, have lots of fun. Realizing that many performing groups may have limited technical and space resources, I have kept sets, costumes and props minimal. However, if you do have the ability to rig up an entire Maidu village for *How the People Got Fire* or build a facsimile flatboat and set of canal locks for *The Most Expensive Bonnet in All Indiana*—go for it! Adding more music and dance and visual arts and crafts into the production involves more children and makes your play a genuinely multimedia event.

Similarly, I have supplied only basic stage and lighting directions. Blocking is really the province of the director; once you get the play up and moving, feel free to suit cast and action to your available population and experience level of actors. When figuring out how to stage these plays, I suggest you follow the venerable UYI Method—Use Your Imagination. If the play calls for a boat, bring in a wood frame, an old bathtub or have children draw a boat and hang as a scrim behind where the actors perform. Keep in mind the spirit of the old Andy Hardy musicals: "C'mon, everybody! Let's make a show!"

Age and gender. Obviously, your purpose in putting on the play is to entertain as well as educate; even though in the historical reality of 1848 a ship's crew would have been all male, there is no reason these roles can't be played in your production by females. After all, the essence of the theatrical experience is to suspend us in time and ask us to believe that anything may be possible. Once again, UYI! Adult characters, such as grandparents or "old mountain men" or "bearded fiddlers," can be played by children costumed or made up to fit the part as closely as possible, or they can actually be played by adults. While *Plays of America for Children* are indeed intended to be performed chiefly by children, moderate adult involvement will add validation and let children know this isn't just a "kid project." If, in a play like *Let's Have a Hoedown!*, you want to get very highly choreographed or musically intensive, you will probably find a strategically placed onstage adult or two very helpful in keeping things moving smoothly.

Plays of America for Children offers the opportunity to learn a little bit more about all of us who make up this amazing nation called the United States of America. And for some adults perhaps, these plays might recapture the joy and excitement we all felt the first time we heard a nursery rhyme and fairy tale. Who says you can't be a kid again? Just put on this coonskin cap, pardner, and meet me at a little spot in San Antone called the Alamo…

L.E. McCullough, Ph.D.
Woodstock, New York

Plays of America
from American Folklore
for Children

HOW THE PEOPLE GOT FIRE

How the People Got Fire is based on a tale from the Maidu tribe of Central California. The Maidu flourished in the coastal country and central valleys north of modern-day San Francisco. They resided in houses made of large earth mounds and lived largely from the bounty of the lush land that surrounded them. The central motif of capturing fire from the gods and bringing it to earth in a flute is widespread in many cultures around the world, recalling the ancient Greek myth of Prometheus, who gave fire to the human race in defiance of the chief god Zeus. Native American tales about the creation of the world typically use animals as protagonists, emphasizing the human race's dependence upon nature for survival and the belief that animals have spirits, as well.

TIME: The dawn of human history

PLACE: In the vast North American desert left by melting glaciers

CAST: Narrator *(Narrator lines can be given to more than one actor.)*
3 Daughters of Thunder & Lightning
Woswosim—big bird, ally of Thunder & Lightning
Toyeskon—small bird, ally of The People
The People (5–10 actors), includes A Mother and A Child

Thunder (male)	Skunk
Lightning (female)	Dog
Lizard	Gopher
Lizard's Brother Frog	Wildcat
Fox	Chipmunk
Deer	Mouse
Coyote	

STAGE SET: barren with some medium-sized boulders to sit on and lean against (painted styrofoam, cardboard), a campfire made of stones in a circle and some kindling sticks

PROPS: a dozen orange-painted rocks to denote embers; a flute (or pennywhistle or recorder); an apron; four corncobs; a spear or club

SPECIAL EFFECTS: thunder, lightning, rain and wind sounds; lightning flashes

1

COSTUMES: all characters can dress in simple one-piece, one-color smocks and sandals; animal masks and headdresses can be made for animal characters; bird characters Woswosim and Toyeskom can be adorned with feathers, Thunder and Lightning and their Three Daughters with raincloud and lightning symbols (the daughters also wear aprons); faces of Narrator and The People can be painted with simple designs based on Native American symbols

(LIGHTS UP STAGE RIGHT, where NARRATOR sits on a rock. He looks at the audience:)

NARRATOR: A long time ago, there was no fire in the world.

(LIGHTS UP HALF STAGE LEFT on THE PEOPLE sitting on the ground, huddled in a circle, shivering.)

NARRATOR: The People who lived in the world then had heard of fire, and they wanted it to keep warm and to cook their food. They had a bird, a small bird named Toyeskom, who had a very bright red eye.

(TOYESKOM enters stage left and is greeted enthusiastically by THE PEOPLE.)

TOYESKOM: I am Toyeskom, my eye is bright and red; with its shiny glare, I help The People to be fed!

(THE PEOPLE guide TOYESKOM to a spot on the ground where four corncobs have been placed.)

NARRATOR: When The People wanted their food cooked, they had Toyeskom turn his bright red eye toward the food, and he would stare at it for a long time. The stare from his bright red eye would make the food warm and cook it.

(TOYESKOM kneels, cocks his head toward the corncobs, shakes and bobs head as if his motions are cooking the food. A CHILD steps forward and addresses its MOTHER.)

NARRATOR: But it took a really long time.

CHILD: Mommy, I am sooooo hungry! When are we ever going to eat?

MOTHER: Patience, my child. Our meal will be cooked in only another few hours.

PEOPLE: *(chanting)* We are The People! We must find fire! We are The People! We must find fire! We are The People! We must find fire!

(TOYESKOM finishes cooking, rises and hands corncobs to PEOPLE, who graciously thank him. LIGHTS DIM ON PEOPLE; LIGHTS UP STAGE RIGHT on THUNDER and LIGHTNING standing motionless.)

NARRATOR: In truth, there was fire in the world, but only Thunder and Lightning, who were married to each other, had it. And they would let no one else have any.

(THUNDER and LIGHTNING dance and twirl to center stage; they drop several fire embers into center of campfire and fall back as fire blazes up.)

THUNDER: I am Thunder, Lord of the World! When I speak my mind, The People tremble and fear!

LIGHTNING: I am Lightning, Thunder's Elegant Queen! When I dance through the heavens, my feet paint the evening sky!

(THUNDER and LIGHTNING'S THREE DAUGHTERS enter from stage right; they each pick up an ember from the fire and put it in their aprons, guarding them carefully.)

NARRATOR: Their daughters kept bits of fire in their aprons, so they would always have plenty.

(THREE DAUGHTERS scurry behind THUNDER and LIGHT-NING and sit; LIGHTS DIM TO HALF and WOSWOSIM enters from stage right, dancing toward campfire. He carries a spear or club, with which he slashes the air and fends off imaginary foes.)

NARRATOR: And at night, when darkness fell, a huge giant bird—Woswosim—guarded the main fire and made sure no one got near to it.

(WOSWOSIM stands guard over fire as THUNDER, LIGHTNING and their THREE DAUGHTERS retire to stage right, lie down and sleep. LIGHTS OUT, A FEW SECONDS PAUSE, THEN UP STAGE LEFT. LIZARD and LIZARD'S BROTHER are stage left, lazily leaning up against boulders.)

NARRATOR: One morning Lizard and his brother were sitting on a rock, sunning themselves. Lizard looked west and was amazed at what he saw.

LIZARD: Brother, look! Over there to the west! What do you see? *(points right)*

LIZARD'S BROTHER: I see...I see...I see smoke!

LIZARD: And?

LIZARD'S BROTHER: And where there is smoke...
LIZARD: Yes?
LIZARD'S BROTHER: There is...there is...there is fire!
LIZARD: Yes! Yes! Yes!

(They hug each other happily and arm-in-arm march toward center; they stop when they see COYOTE, who has entered from stage right.)

NARRATOR: Lizard and his brother ran back home. On the way they saw Coyote.

LIZARD & LIZARD'S BROTHER: Coyote! Coyote! Guess what we have seen?

COYOTE: Oh, it's you lizards again! What is it this time?

LIZARD: We have seen fire!

COYOTE: Fire?

LIZARD'S BROTHER: Smoke, actually.

COYOTE: Smoke?

LIZARD: But where there is smoke—

LIZARD'S BROTHER: There is fire!

(LIZARD and his brother jump up and down excitedly, but COYOTE is unimpressed.)

COYOTE: Listen, Coyote is the Trickster around here. *I* am the one who makes up jokes and pranks. You can't kid a kidder. Smoke! Fire! I don't believe a word you lizards say!

LIZARD & LIZARD'S BROTHER: *(they point right)* Look!

(COYOTE turns, sees smoke and is startled.)

COYOTE: It is smoke! And it is coming from the land where Thunder and Lightning live. Quick, lizards, we must call the other animals at once! *(turns and looks stage left to where THE PEOPLE sit huddled)* We must get fire to The People.

LIZARD & LIZARD'S BROTHER: Calling all animals! Calling all animals! Come meet with Coyote at once!

(FROG, FOX, SNAKE, WILDCAT, MOUSE, DEER, DOG, CHIP-MUNK and SKUNK enter from stage right as their names are called,

dancing briefly or miming their animal gaits before gathering around COYOTE and LIZARD and LIZARD'S BROTHER.)

NARRATOR: And in awhile, all the animals of the World came: Frog...Fox...Snake...Wildcat...Mouse...Deer...Dog...Chipmunk...Skunk.

COYOTE: Animals of the World, we have seen smoke!

LIZARD: And where there is smoke—

LIZARD'S BROTHER: There is fire!

ANIMALS: *(cheer)* Hurrah! They have seen smoke! They have seen fire!

COYOTE: Quiet, please. This smoke and fire belong to Thunder and Lightning.

ANIMALS: *(moans)* Oh, no...not Thunder and Lightning.

MOUSE: We must get this fire and bring it to The People.

FROG: That will not be easy. They say an evil bird, Woswosim, guards the fire at night. He never sleeps.

WILDCAT: That is no problem. *(mimes motions)* I, Wildcat, will creep up on this evil bird and devour him before he has time to say "one, two, three"!

DEER: The noise would wake Thunder and Lightning and their Three Daughters. You would never come back alive.

SNAKE: Wait! How about if *I* sneak up and bite this Woswoswim in the ankle?

DOG: You would be crushed when he fell on you. You would never bring fire back.

CHIPMUNK: I know! I will face this giant bird.

FOX: You? You're a little teeny chipmunk!

CHIPMUNK: I *know* what I am, Fox! I am a chipmunk—a chipmunk who plays the *flute.*

(CHIPMUNK takes out a flute and plays a sweet melody; animals sigh and swoon.)

SKUNK: That is truly beautiful. Chipmunk can play his flute and make Woswosim fall asleep. That will give us a chance to take the fire.

(Animals mutter their assent; LIGHTS DIM, A FEW SECONDS PAUSE, THEN UP TO HALF STAGE RIGHT where THUNDER

and LIGHTNING and their THREE DAUGHTERS are asleep in the corner. WOSWOSIM stands to the right of their campfire, spreading his wings and pacing slowly to and fro.)

WOSWOSIM: I, giant Woswosim, am the fiercest bird in the sky! I am so strong that I never sleep! Only babies sleep! I never sleep, and no one in the world can defeat me!

(CHIPMUNK, MOUSE, DOG, COYOTE and DEER have crept up from stage left, hiding themselves behind boulders. CHIPMUNK takes out his flute and begins to play softly. SOUND CUE: flute music.)

WOSWOSIM: *(jumps up, alert)* What sound is that? Who disturbs the campfire of Thunder and Lightning?

(CHIPMUNK stops; other animals shrink back. After a pause, CHIP-MUNK plays again.)

WOSWOSIM: *(relaxes)* Hmmm. Must be some kind of bird. A night bird like me. Well, you can't have too many *me* around the world.

(As the music continues, WOSWOSIM sits, gets comfortable against a rock, nods his head.)

WOSWOSIM: *(yawns)* That is a very pretty melody. *(yawns)* So very… very…very… *(falls asleep)*

(CHIPMUNK stops playing, other animals enter campsite as described below.)

NARRATOR: When the animals saw that Woswosim had fallen asleep, they sprang into action. Mouse untied the Three Daughters' aprons and took their fire. He put some fire in Dog's ear, some in Coyote's mouth and the rest in the flute. He gave the flute to Deer, being the swiftest runner. But then, all of a sudden, Thunder and Lightning awoke.

THUNDER: What is going on?

LIGHTNING: Who are all these animals?

THREE DAUGHTERS: Our aprons are untied! They've stolen our fire!

THUNDER: They've stolen all the fire! Thieves!

LIGHTNING: Woswosim, wake up! After them!

(The animals scatter across stage, ducking and covering, guarding their fire; WOSWOSIM stands in campfire, flapping his wings; THUNDER and LIGHTNING and their THREE DAUGHTERS begin dancing, creating big rainstorms with wind and hail and terrible lightning. SOUND CUE: thunder, lightning, rain and wind sounds. LIGHT EFFECTS: lightning flashes.)

NARRATOR: Thunder and Lightning gave chase. They danced and danced in the sky and made big winds and rainstorms that shook the world, from one end to the other.

(CHIPMUNK, MOUSE, DOG, COYOTE and DEER reel and tumble, struggle to get up; THUNDER, LIGHTNING, THREE DAUGH-TERS and WOSWOSIM stalk them.)

NARRATOR: But just as Thunder and Lightning and their Three Daughters were about to catch up with the animals…Skunk rushed in to the fray.

(SKUNK jumps between animals and pursuers; facing THUNDER and LIGHTNING, he throws forth his arms as if casting a net.)

NARRATOR: And he sent toward them a mighty blast of his own wind…a powerful wind all skunks command even to this day, when they battle a bigger foe.

(THUNDER, LIGHTNING, THREE DAUGHTERS and WOS-WOSIM fall down, shrink back, coughing, rubbing eyes.)

THUNDER & LIGHTNING: Stop! Stop! No more, skunk! Stop! This wind is killing us!

SKUNK: I will stop. But only if you promise that after today, you must never try to take fire from The People.

THUNDER & LIGHTNING: *(groveling)* We promise! We promise!

SKUNK: I accept your promise and your word you will keep it. Forever more, you must stay up in the sky and be thunder and be lightning. That is where you must be.

(THUNDER and LIGHTNING and their THREE DAUGHTERS and WOSWOSIM mumble and shake their heads in assent, exiting

slowly right. LIGHTS UP LEFT on THE PEOPLE, standing now, looking up and excitedly pointing at the sky.)

NARRATOR: And so the animals returned to the world with fire, which they gave to The People.

(Animals hand fire embers to THE PEOPLE; THE PEOPLE thank them profusely. The animals creep, crawl, flutter, scamper offstage right while THE PEOPLE place embers into their new campfire, then gather in a semicircle round the fire and sit, hold hands, lie down, sleep as LIGHTS DIM.)

NARRATOR: And The People have had it ever since.

(LIGHTS OUT.)

THE END

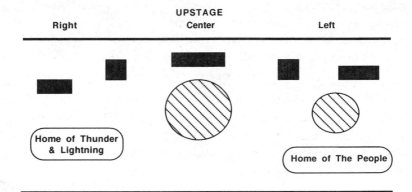

Stage Plan *How the People Got Fire*

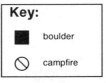

LET'S HAVE A HOEDOWN!

Let's Have a Hoedown! showcases the folklore and history contained in several popular 19th-century songs and dance tunes, music that became a staple element of the "old-time country music" played at square and contra dances throughout America today.

For best musical results, the character of Grandpa (or Grandma, if desired) should be played by an actual adult to help direct the dancing activity—basic square dancing, jigging and clogging. The instrument can be banjo, fiddle, mandolin, guitar, accordion or piano. If an adult or teen actor with musical ability is not available, recorded music can be used and actors can lip-synch and mime.

TIME: Right now!

PLACE: A living room, Anytown, U.S.A.

CAST: Grandpa (or Grandma)   Yellow Rose of Texas
         Jeff   Soldier
         Jessica   Arkansas Traveler
         Sailor   Farmer
         Old Joe Clark   Susanna
         Old Joe's Dog   Minstrel
         Old Joe's Horse   Simon Slick
         Old Joe's Wife   Simon Slick's Mule
         John Henry   Young Man Who Wouldn't Hoe Corn
         The Captain   Pretty Little Miss
         Old Dan Tucker   8 Square Dancers

STAGE SET: a wooden folding chair for Grandpa at stage right; if desired, a small living room set could be created (table, bookcase, lamp) and American history posters hung along rear curtain, but the stage should preferably be kept as clear as possible to accommodate the large number of actors

PROPS: sledge hammer; hand power drill (unplugged); hoe; rolling pin; harmonica; 5-string banjo; frying pan; papier-mache wagon wheel

COSTUMES: Grandpa, Jeff and Jessica dress contemporary casual; others wear 19th-century rural garb or dress as described in song (i.e., Sailor wears old-style sailor outfit)

(LIGHTS UP stage right on a living room where GRANDPA sits, strumming the 5-string banjo. His twin grandkids, JEFF AND JESSICA, approach from left and GRANDPA stops playing to greet them.)

GRANDPA: Hello, Jeff! Hello, Jessica!

JEFF & JESSICA: Hi, Grandpa!

JEFF: Gosh, Grandpa, that music you play on the banjo is really neat!

JESSICA: It makes me want to dance!

GRANDPA: Well, that's what it's supposed to do. It's music made for dancing.

JEFF: Who made it?

GRANDPA: Folks just like you. Folks whose parents came to America two and three hundred years ago from all around the world. And though they came here to work and settle the countryside, they also liked to have fun. So they brought their music with them. Why, to a young man or woman on the frontier a hundred years back, a banjo or a fiddle was as important a tool as a rake or a hoe.

JESSICA: Where did the banjo come from?

GRANDPA: The American banjo was patterned after an instrument first made in Africa and brought over to America by Africans in the 1600s. Other Americans picked it up, and now, it's part of the music all Americans play. It's called "folk music," and it's one of the best ways there is to learn about people and their history.

JEFF: But all that folk music sounds the same to me. How can you tell any of it apart?

GRANDPA: Same way I tell you and your sister apart! I look for what's special about you. Every folk song has its own story behind it…about the people and the place and time they lived. If all folk songs sound the same to you, my boy, that's just because you don't know their stories. Listen to this:

(GRANDPA plays The Sailor's Hornpipe.*)*

JESSICA: I know that song! It's *Popeye, the Sailor Man!*

GRANDPA: That's true, but this song was around a long time before they had Popeye cartoons. Its real title is *The Sailor's Hornpipe*, and it was composed over two hundred years ago in England. That's the time when the English navy ruled the seven seas, and at theatre shows, between the acts of a play, actors dressed like sailors would come out and dance. Oh, the audience loved it!

(SAILOR enters from left and dances a hornpipe as GRANDPA plays The Sailor's Hornpipe; exits left when finished.)

GRANDPA: Listen. And look. *(points left)* Here comes somebody you might recognize from down South—Old Joe Clark.

(GRANDPA plays Old Joe Clark; OLD JOE CLARK enters from left, clogging, followed by A DOG, A HORSE and A WOMAN who mime actions in song at center stage.)

GRANDPA: *(sings)*
Old Joe Clark had a house, it was sixteen stories high
And every room in that house smelled like chicken pie
(speaks) Here's the chorus, kids: come on and sing along!
GRANDPA, JEFF & JESSICA: *(sing)*
Round and around, Old Joe Clark, round and around we're gone
Round and around, Old Joe Clark, and bye-bye Lucy Long
GRANDPA: *(sings)*
Old Joe Clark, he had a dog as blind as he could be
Ran a redbug round a stump and a squirrel up a tree
GRANDPA, JEFF & JESSICA: *(sing)*
Round and around, Old Joe Clark, round and around we're gone
Round and around, Old Joe Clark, and bye-bye Lucy Long
GRANDPA: *(sings)*
Old Joe Clark had a horse, his name was Morgan Brown
And everywhere Old Joe went, he covered an acre of ground
GRANDPA, JEFF & JESSICA: *(sing)*
Round and around, Old Joe Clark, round and around we're gone
Round and around, Old Joe Clark, and bye-bye Lucy Long
GRANDPA: *(sings)*
Old Joe Clark he had a wife, and she was seven feet tall
She slept with her head in the kitchen and her feet in the hall
GRANDPA, JEFF & JESSICA: *(sing)*
Round and around, Old Joe Clark, round and around we're gone
Round and around, Old Joe Clark, and bye-bye Lucy Long

GRANDPA: *(sings)*
> Old Joe Clark is dead and gone, I'll tell you the reason why
> He ate a barrel of sauerkraut and drank the river dry

GRANDPA, JEFF & JESSICA: *(sing)*
> Round and around, Old Joe Clark, round and around we're gone
> Round and around, Old Joe Clark, and bye-bye Lucy Long

(OLD JOE CLARK, DOG, HORSE and WOMAN exit left; THE YELLOW ROSE OF TEXAS and A SOLDIER enter from right, go to center.)

JEFF: Who's that, Grandpa?

GRANDPA: Why, that lady is one of the most famous women in American history. When Texas was fighting Mexico for its independence in 1836, it was The Yellow Rose who saved the day for Texas at the Battle of San Jacinto.

(EIGHT SQUARE DANCERS enter from stage left; form a square next to YELLOW ROSE and SOLDIER.)

JESSICA: Look! Square dancers! It's a hoedown!

(GRANDPA plays The Yellow Rose of Texas; *SQUARE DANCERS dance a set; YELLOW ROSE and SOLDIER dance with each other.)*

GRANDPA: *(sings)*
> There's a yellow rose in Texas that I am going to see
> No other soldier knows her, no other, only me
> She cried so when I left her, it like to broke my heart
> And if I ever find her, we never more will part

JEFF & JESSICA: *(sing)*
> When the Rio Grande is flowing and the starry skies are bright
> She walks along the river in the quiet summer night
> She thinks if I remember how we parted long ago
> I promised to come back again and not to leave her so

GRANDPA, JEFF & JESSICA: *(sing)*
> She's the sweetest little flower this soldier ever knew
> Her eyes are bright as diamonds, they sparkle like the dew
> You may talk about your dearest May and sing of Rosa Lee
> But the Yellow Rose of Texas beats the Belles of Tennessee

GRANDPA: *(sings)*

And now I'm going to find her, for my heart is full of woe
We'll sing the song together, that we sung so long ago

GRANDPA, JEFF & JESSICA: *(sing)*

We'll play the banjo gaily, and we'll sing the songs of yore
And the Yellow Rose of Texas shall be mine forevermore

(YELLOW ROSE and SOLDIER exit right; SQUARE DANCERS remain at left, sitting on floor as JOHN HENRY and THE CAPTAIN enter from left; JOHN HENRY holds a sledgehammer, THE CAPTAIN a power drill; during ensuing dialogue JOHN HENRY wields hammer, CAPTAIN watches with envy.)

GRANDPA: A lot of folk songs are about ordinary people who do extraordinary things. Like the railroad worker John Henry, who lived in West Virginia in the 1870s. He was just about the strongest man this country has ever seen. Why, he could tunnel through a mountain all by himself! But came a time, the railroad builders wanted to use machines to do the work instead of men, so John Henry set out to prove that a man was just as good as any piece of metal.

(GRANDPA plays John Henry; DANCERS watch and clap, join in with JEFF and JESSICA on last line of each verse as JOHN HENRY and THE CAPTAIN do song actions.)

GRANDPA: *(sings)*

John Henry was a little baby sitting on his mama's knee
Said, "The Big Bend Tunnel on the C and O Road
Gonna cause the death of me, Lord, Lord
Gonna cause the death of me"

Captain says to John Henry, "Bring me a steam drill round
Gonna take that steam drill on the job
Gonna hammer that steel on down, Lord, Lord
Gonna hammer that steel on down"

John Henry told the captain—lightning was in his eye
"Captain, bet your last red cent on me
For I'll beat it to the bottom or I'll die, Lord, Lord
I'll beat it to the bottom or I'll die"

The man that invented the steam drill thought he was mighty fine
John Henry drove his hammer fifteen feet
And the steam drill only made nine, Lord, Lord
And the steam drill only made nine

John Henry told his captain, "Look yonder at what I see
Your drill's done broke and your hole's done choke
And you can't drive steel like me, Lord, Lord
No, you can't drive steel like me"

Well every Monday morning when the bluebirds begin to sing
You can hear those hammers a mile or more
You can hear John Henry's hammer ring, Lord, Lord
You can hear John Henry's hammer ring

(JOHN HENRY and THE CAPTAIN exit right; FARMER enters from left, followed to center stage by ARKANSAS TRAVELER; FARMER toots on harmonica after answering the TRAVELER'S questions.)

ARKANSAS TRAVELER: Hello, Farmer!

FARMER: Hello yourself, Traveler. *(plays harmonica)*

ARKANSAS TRAVELER: Say, where's this road go to?

FARMER: Don't go anywhere; just always stays right there. *(plays)*

ARKANSAS TRAVELER: Am I in the State of Arkansas?

FARMER: Sounds like you're in the State of Confusion. *(plays)*

ARKANSAS TRAVELER: Well, how far is it to the next house?

FARMER: Don't know, never been there. *(plays)*

ARKANSAS TRAVELER: It looks like it's going to rain; can I stay in your house tonight?

FARMER: Can't; roof leaks. *(plays)*

ARKANSAS TRAVELER: Why don't you fix it?

FARMER: Cause it's going to rain. *(plays)*

ARKANSAS TRAVELER: Why don't you fix it when it's not raining?

FARMER: When it's not raining, it doesn't leak. *(plays)*

ARKANSAS TRAVELER: Say, why don't you play the second part of that tune?

FARMER: Don't know it.

ARKANSAS TRAVELER: Well, give that harmonica to me, and I'll show you!

(He [or GRANDPA] plays the second part of Arkansas Traveler *and sets FARMER dancing; SUSANNA and A MINSTREL carrying a banjo enter from left and stand center; ARKANSAS TRAVELER and FARMER step back and join SQUARE DANCERS who rise and clap along as MINSTREL plays* Oh, Susanna.*)*

MINSTREL: *(sings)*
> I come from Alabama with a banjo on my knee
> I'm going to Louisiana, my true love for to see

ALL: *(sing)*
> Oh, Susanna, oh, don't you cry for me
> I come from Alabama with a banjo on my knee

SUSANNA: *(sings)*
> I had a dream the other night when everything was still
> I dreamed I saw my true love there a-coming down the hill

ALL: *(sing)*
> Oh, Susanna, oh, don't you cry for me
> I come from Alabama with a banjo on my knee

MINSTREL: *(sings)*
> It rained all night the day I left, the weather it was dry
> The sun so hot I froze to death, Susanna don't you cry

ALL: *(sing)*
> Oh, Susanna, oh, don't you cry for me
> I come from Alabama with a banjo on my knee

SUSANNA: *(sings)*
> A red red rose was in my cheek, a tear was in my eye
> He said to me, "Susanna girl, Susanna don't you cry"

ALL: *(sing)*
> Oh, Susanna, oh, don't you cry for me
> I come from Alabama with a banjo on my knee

(SUSANNA and MINSTREL step back behind SQUARE DANCERS as SIMON SLICK and SIMON SLICK'S MULE enter from left, cross to center and mime song actions during the song Simon Slick.*)*

JEFF: Aw, Grandpa, that never happened! How could anybody freeze to death in the sun?

JESSICA: That's just a silly old song!

GRANDPA: Is that so? Well, here's a song that's even sillier!
GRANDPA: *(sings)*

    There was a man lived in this town, his name was Simon Slick
    He had a mule with dreamy eyes and how that mule could kick
    He'd shut his eye and shake his tail and greet you with a smile
    Then he'd send a telegraph with his leg and kick you half a mile

ALL: *(sing)*

    Whoa, mule, whoa! Whoa, mule, whoa!
    Every time that mule turns round, it's whoa, mule, whoa!

GRANDPA: *(sings)*

    He kicked the feathers off a goose and pulverized a hog
    Dissected seven senators and whupped a yellow dog
    He bit a calico cat in two and broke an elephant's back
    Then he stopped a Texas railroad train and kicked it off the track

ALL: *(sing)*

    Whoa, mule, whoa! Whoa, mule, whoa!
    Every time that mule turns round, it's whoa, mule, whoa!

GRANDPA: *(sings)*

    He stopped a steamboat with his head and kicked it out of sight
    Then he kicked a skating rink in two at nine o'clock one night
    He left those skaters on their heads a-gasping for their breath
    Then he poked a hind leg down his throat and kick himself to death

ALL: *(sing)*

    Whoa, mule, whoa! Whoa, mule, whoa!
    Every time that mule turns round, it's whoa, mule, whoa!

(SIMON SLICK and SIMON SLICK'S MULE exit right; YOUNG MAN WHO WOULDN'T HOE CORN and PRETTY LITTLE MISS enter from left, he carrying a hoe, she a rolling pin.)

JESSICA: I guess that's why they invented tractors, huh, Grandpa?
GRANDPA: Well, farming was and is mighty hard work. But it's not just mules that get contrary. Here's a song about the laziest man there ever was— *The Young Man Who Wouldn't Hoe Corn.*
GRANDPA: *(sings)*

    I'll sing you a song and it's not very long
    About a young man who wouldn't hoe corn

The reason why I cannot tell
For this young man was always well, this young man was always well

He planted his corn in the month of June
And in July it was knee high
First of September came a big frost
All this young man's corn was lost, all this young man's corn was lost

He went to the fence and there peeped in
The weeds and the grass came up to his chin
The weeds and the grass they grew so high
Caused this young man for to sigh, caused this young man for to sigh

So he went down to his neighbor's door
Where he'd often been before
"Pretty little miss, will you marry me
Pretty little miss what do you say? Pretty little miss what do you say?"

"Here you are wanting to wed
But you cannot make your own cornbread
Single I am and single I'll remain
A lazy man I'll not maintain, a lazy man I'll not maintain"

(YOUNG MAN and PRETTY LITTLE MISS step back alongside other characters; GRANDPA stands and addresses JEFF and JESSICA.)

GRANDPA: Well, it's probably time you two got back to your homework.

JEFF: Gee, Grandpa, this has been a neat history lesson.

JESSICA:I never knew folk music could tell you so much about history.

GRANDPA: Folk music *is* history. It's the living history of a country and its people. Even today, men, women and children all over America—all over the world, in fact—are composing songs and tunes about the things that are important in their daily life…even if it's sometimes just about the silly people they know. Look! Here comes Old Dan Tucker from the rodeo!

(OLD DAN TUCKER, a clown/bumpkin-type, enters from left carrying a frying pan and a wagon wheel, followed by the YELLOW ROSE OF TEXAS, SOLDIER, SAILOR, OLD JOE CLARK, OLD JOE'S

DOG, OLD JOE'S HORSE, OLD JOE'S WIFE, JOHN HENRY, THE CAPTAIN, SIMON SLICK and SIMON SLICK'S MULE; everyone sings and claps along (encourage audience to join in on chorus) as OLD DAN TUCKER clogs and mimes his lyric actions during the song Old Dan Tucker.*)*

ALL: *(sing)*

Old Dan Tucker's a fine old man; washed his face in a frying pan
Combed his head with a wagon wheel; died with a toothache in his heel

Get out the way, Old Dan Tucker; you're too late to get your supper
Supper's over and dinner's cookin'; Old Dan Tucker just stands there lookin'

Old Dan Tucker came to town, riding a billygoat and leading a hound
Hound it barked and the billygoat jumped; threw old Dan right into a stump

Get out the way, Old Dan Tucker; you're too late to get your supper
Supper's over and dinner's cookin'; Old Dan Tucker just stands there lookin'

Old Dan Tucker he came to town, swinging the ladies round and round
First to the right and then to the left; then to the one that you love best

Get out the way, Old Dan Tucker; you're too late to get your supper
Supper's over and dinner's cookin'; Old Dan Tucker just stands there lookin'

Get out the way, Old Dan Tucker; you're too late to get your supper
Supper's over and dinner's cookin'; Old Dan Tucker just stands there lookin'

(Music ends; all clap; LIGHTS OUT.)

THE END

Sailor's Hornpipe

Old Joe Clark

Old Joe Clark had a house it was six- teen stor- ies high and

eve- ry room in that house smelled like chick- en pie

Round and a- round, Old Joe Clark, round and a- round we're gone

Round and a- round, Old Joe Clark, and good- bye Lu- cy Long

The Yellow Rose of Texas

There's a yel- low rose in Tex- as that I am going to see No oth- er sol- dier knows her, no oth- er, on- ly me She cried so when I left her, it like to broke my heart And if I ev- er find her, we ne- ver more will part

John Henry

John Hen- ry was a lit- tle ba- by sit- ting on his ma- ma's knee Said, "The Big Bend Tun- nel on the C and O- o Road Gon- na cause the death of me, lord, lord Gon- na cause the death of me"

Arkansas Traveler

Oh, Susanna

I come from Al- a- ba- ma with a ban- jo on my knee I'm going to Louis- i- a- na, my true love for to see Oh, Su- san- na, oh, don't you cry for me I come from Al- a- ba- ma with a ban- jo on my knee

Simon Slick

There was a man lived in this town his name was Si-mon
Slick He had a mule with drea-my eyes and how that mule could
kick He'd shut his eye and shake his tail and greet you with a
smile Then he'd send a te-le-graph with his leg and kick you half a
smile Whoa, mule, whoa! Whoa, mule, whoa! Eve-ry time that
mule turns round, it's whoa, mule, whoa!

The Young Man Who Wouldn't Hoe Corn

I'll sing you a song and it's not ve-ry long a-bout a young
man who would-n't hoe corn The rea-son why I can-not
tell For this young man was al-ways well, this young man was al-ways
well

Old Dan Tucker

Old Dan Tuck-er's a fine old man; washed his face in a fry- ing pan

Combed his head with a wa- gon wheel; died with a tooth- ache in his heel

Get out the way, Old Dan Tuck- er; you're too late to get your sup- per

Sup- per's o- ver and din- ner's cook- in'; Old Dan Tuck-er just stands there look-in'

THE COBBLER'S PIPE

The Cobbler's Pipe is based on a tale from the early days of Dutch settlement in New York. The original St. Nicholas was the bishop of Myra in Asia Minor during the 4th century A.D. Several of the miracles ascribed to him involved helping and caring for children, and he is one of the many ancient figures who became part of our modern legend of Santa Claus. In Dutch folklore, St. Nicholas (Sant Nikolaas) is a plump, jolly old man who brings gifts to children and needy families on his feast day, December 6. The night before, children fill wooden shoes with hay and sugar and leave them out for St. Nicholas and his horse; when they wake up the next morning, the hay and sugar are gone, and the shoes are filled with cakes and sweets. Later that day, St. Nicholas returns with presents.

TIME: December, 1660

PLACE: The Dutch Colony of New Amsterdam (New York City)

CAST:

Frau Kiersted	Customer
Jan	Heer Hommel
Anneke	A Stranger
Cobbler Claas	4 City Councilmen
Frau Claas	4 Road Builders
4 Claas Children	4 Soldiers

STAGE SET: downstage—a rocking chair; a table and four stools; a bench; a curtain and a table behind the curtain; upstage in front of back curtain—full-size panels with drawings of a plush house interior (a rack of clothes, a long mirror, fancy sitting chairs, a wooden dresser, etc.)

PROPS: knitting and knitting needles; cobbler's hammer; a pair of boots; a shoe with nails in the sole; blueprints; large stick rulers; shovel; a teapot; a fruit bowl containing two ears of corn and four potatoes; gold coins; polishing rag; Bible with silver clasps; a big meerschaum pipe with curved stem and large bowl; thin wood (or bamboo) cane; food platters, bread loaf, turkey, pudding, pie; wrapped presents; a piece of paper

COSTUMES: late 17th-century Dutch dress for all characters; for detail, look at paintings by Rembrandt, Rubens, Van Dyck, Berchem, etc.

(LIGHTS UP STAGE RIGHT, where FRAU KIERSTED sits in a rocking chair, knitting and humming a Christmas song, We Three Kings of Orient Are. *She stops knitting and gazes out toward audience.)*

FRAU KIERSTED: My goodness! Look at that snow! It is coming down like a shower of geese!

(SOUND: KNOCKING ON DOOR FROM STAGE LEFT; two children, the boy JAN and the girl ANNEKE, bound in from stage left and kneel on either side of FRAU KIERSTED.)

JAN & ANNEKE: Frau Kiersted! Frau Kiersted!

FRAU KIERSTED: Jan! Anneke! How are you this cold December day?

JAN: We are fine. But we want to know how many days it is until Christmas.

ANNEKE: And we want to know where St. Nicholas lives, so we can send a letter to him asking for gifts.

FRAU KIERSTED: *(chuckles)* Well, perhaps that is something you should ask your parents, not a simple seamstress like me. And what makes you so certain St. Nicholas is going to bring any gifts to *you* children?

JAN: We have been very good all year.

ANNEKE: We have done very well with our lessons in school.

JAN: And I have not pulled Anneke's hair once—well, not since Midsummer's Eve.

FRAU KIERSTED: *(pats their heads)* That *is* very good, children. But doing only what is expected of you is not enough to please St. Nicholas.

ANNEKE: What else should we do?

FRAU KIERSTED: Did you ever hear of the cobbler named Claas? Well, he lived right here in New York City, back in the days when it was called New Amsterdam, about the year 1660.

(LIGHTS UP STAGE CENTER AND STAGE LEFT; the COBBLER CLAAS enters from stage left and walks buoyantly to his work bench, stage center; he picks up a cobbler's hammer and begins working on a pair of boots. A CUSTOMER enters from stage right and approaches COBBLER CLAAS.)

CUSTOMER: Cobbler Claas! Have you finished my new boots?

COBBLER CLAAS: Here they are, good sir.

CUSTOMER: *(examines them)* Why, you are the very best cobbler in all of New Amsterdam! How did you become such a fine cobbler?

COBBLER CLAAS: When I came to America from Holland, I was a poor orphan boy. In order to pay for my ship passage, I was indentured for seven years as an apprentice to a master cobbler. I helped him with his work, and he taught me everything he knew about making boots and shoes. I worked hard and, after many years, finally saved enough money to open my own cobbler shop.

CUSTOMER: And now you are one of the wealthiest citizens of New Amsterdam. You have a lovely brick house with a garden and a big pond of fat white geese.

COBBLER CLAAS: But the most precious thing I have, good sir, is my family: my loving wife Anitje and my four young children.

(FRAU CLAAS and FOUR CLAAS CHILDREN enter from stage right and go to COBBLER CLAAS, hugging him and bowing and curtsying to CUSTOMER.)

CUSTOMER: Yes, indeed, cobbler, you have been greatly blessed. Good day!

(He exits left with boots. FRAU CLAAS and COBBLER CLAAS prepare the CLAAS CHILDREN for an outing; they straighten the children's clothes, brush their hair; from behind curtain at stage left, HEER HOMMEL crouches and peeks out, scowling.)

FRAU KIERSTED: Although the Cobbler Claas had many blessings, he also had a great enemy. The town burgomaster, Heer Hommel, was the richest man in New Amsterdam, and he deeply resented the successful orphan boy. When Claas and his family took walks through the town, Heer Hommel hid behind the curtains of his house and thought terrible things. One day, he put his ugly thoughts into evil deeds.

(THE CLAAS FAMILY walks left across the stage in front of HEER HOMMEL; they smile and laugh and wave, exiting left. HEER HOMMEL emerges from behind curtain, walks to bench and picks up Claas'

cobbler hammer; from his jacket, he pulls out a shoe with nails driven in the sole.)

HEER HOMMEL: *(brandishes hammer and shoe)* I will teach the village blacksmith to make hobnails for the people's boots. *(bangs shoe on table)* The nails will make a dreadful noise as people walk over the brick streets. But they will also keep the boots from wearing out so soon, and the Cobbler Claas will not have so much business for new boots!

(He laughs wickedly, puts down hobnailed shoe and hammer, exits right. COBBLER CLAAS, FRAU CLAAS and CLAAS CHILDREN enter from stage left, smiling and waving, and walk to table that has a teapot and a fruit bowl containing two ears of corn and four potatoes; the children sit, and COBBLER CLAAS picks up hobnailed shoe and sighs at FRAU CLAAS.)

FRAU KIERSTED: Even though the Cobbler had a hard time making ends meet, he and his family still lived in their nice brick home and took walks through town in their fine handsome clothes. Heer Hommel had to think of something else.

(HEER HOMMEL enters from stage right followed by FOUR BUILDERS, who carry rulers and blueprints and shovel. THE BUILDERS walk around the CLAAS FAMILY, measuring them and the table; one of the BUILDERS begins shoveling to left of table.)

COBBLER CLAAS: Heer Hommel, what are you doing to our yard?

HEER HOMMEL: Cobbler Claas, the city of New Amsterdam is growing. As town burgomaster, I have ordered a new street to be built.

COBBLER CLAAS: Through the middle of our geese pond?

HEER HOMMEL: Would you rather have it through the middle of your house? Carry on, builders! *(exits right)*

FRAU CLAAS: This is terrible, husband! We sold the eggs to make up for the money you no longer earn from selling boots. Now we will have to sell our geese!

(FOUR BUILDERS and CLAAS CHILDREN exit right; FOUR CITY COUNCILMEN enter from stage left, advance to COBBLER CLAAS and stand before him.)

COUNCILMAN #1: As Councilmen for the city of New Amsterdam, we thank you for the use of your property to build our new street.

COBBLER CLAAS: I suppose it is an honor, of sorts.

COUNCILMAN #2: And, since the street runs through *your* property, you must pay for its construction.

COBBLER CLAAS: What?

COUNCILMAN #3: The construction fee is fifty gold gilders!

COBBLER CLAAS: Fifty gold gilders! That is all the money we have in the world!

COUNCILMAN #4: That will do, then.

(FRAU CLAAS reaches into the teapot and gives coins to COUNCIL-MAN #4; COUNCILMEN exit left. COBBLER CLAAS picks up hammer and sits at bench, hammering air; FRAU CLAAS takes a rag and polishes fruit bowl.)

FRAU KIERSTED: The cobbler and his wife had to work harder and harder to keep their family clothed and fed. For awhile they sold vegetables from their little garden and managed to scrape by.

(FOUR BUILDERS enter from right with blueprints, rulers and shovel and stand to left of COBBLER and wife.)

FRAU KIERSTED: But the burgomaster ordered another street to be built—this time through the middle of the Claas Family's garden patch.

(HEER HOMMEL enters from right, bows and takes fruit bowl from table; he turns and exits right, laughing; BUILDERS take down panel drawings and remove them, exiting left, until all are removed; CITY COUNCILMEN enter from left and carry off table stools, exiting right.)

FRAU KIERSTED: And so it continued. Every time Claas and his wife made a little money, Heer Hommel ordered a new road built and made the Claas family pay for it. Finally, the little family had sold their house and almost all their belongings just to keep alive. When Christmas Eve came that year, the Cobbler and his family lived in a miserable little cottage.

(COBBLER CLAAS and FRAU CLAAS sit on bench; CLAAS CHIL-DREN enter from right and sit on floor in front of parents, facing audience. They all stare sorrowfully in front of them.)

CLAAS CHILD #1: Mama? Do we have any more bread and cheese? I'm hungry!

FRAU CLAAS: I'm sorry. We have no food left at all. Not even a crumb.

CLAAS CHILD #2: Papa, I'm cold!

COBBLER CLAAS: That is the last log we have burning in the fireplace now. You children huddle together. You'll keep warmer that way.

(CHILDREN huddle together, put their heads between their knees. FRAU CLAAS gets up and goes over to the table; she opens a drawer and pulls out a book with silver clasps.)

COBBLER CLAAS: Wife, what are you doing with that Bible?

FRAU CLAAS: We can sell these silver clasps and get enough money to have a small Christmas for the children.

COBBLER CLAAS: No! Your mother gave that to us for our wedding present. It would be better to starve than to feast from the sale of a holy thing.

FRAU CLAAS: Then what will we do?

(COBBLER CLAAS rises and goes to table drawer; he pulls out a meerschaum pipe.)

COBBLER CLAAS: We have one more treasure. When I was a little boy, leaving my home in Holland for the New World, I found this pipe underneath my pillow.

FRAU CLAAS: Where did it come from?

COBBLER CLAAS: I do not know. Perhaps it came from St. Nicholas. *(laughs and rubs it against his sleeve)* It has never been smoked. But I bet it will fetch a few gilders at the market. *(rubs it against his sleeve)*

(SOUND: KNOCKING ON DOOR FROM STAGE LEFT; COB-BLER CLAAS walks over to curtain, and A STRANGER jumps from behind the curtain and strolls past the Cobbler to center stage. The Stranger has a long white beard, a white stocking cap and a red frock coat; he carries a thin wood cane. The CHILDREN get down behind the table, and FRAU CLAAS stands nervously behind her husband.)

STRANGER: *(shivers)* Brrrrr! It's about time you answered the door! I have very nearly turned into an icicle! Come along, why don't you put another log on the fire? Can't you see I am half-frozen?

COBBLER CLAAS: I am very sorry, good sir. But we have no more logs to put on the fire.

STRANGER: No more logs? Nonsense! Oh, very well…I'll do it myself!

(THE STRANGER breaks his cane over his knee and tosses it on the floor in front of him; the Claas family falls back in amazement.)

FRAU CLAAS: Husband! The pieces of cane have become big logs!

COBBLER CLAAS: The fire is blazing away!

STRANGER: There, that's better. And now I suppose you are going to let me starve to death as well?

FRAU CLAAS: Good sir, had we any more food, we should be happy to give you our last crumb.

COBBLER CLAAS: But we have nothing. Not even a morsel.

STRANGER: Well, that is certainly rude! I come to your house after a hard day's tramp over the mountains, through wind and rain and snow! You have no fire to warm me, and now you say you have no food! Well, I know better! *(He walks to curtain and points to it.)* Your pantry is *full* of food! And, if that isn't roast goose I'm smelling, I'll eat my beard!

(COBBLER and FRAU CLAAS go to curtain and pull it back; there sits a table laden with food; wrapped presents are piled underneath; THE CHILDREN run over.)

CHILD #3: Look! There are presents!

CHILD #4: And all this food!

STRANGER: Well, what are you waiting for? Dig in!

(THE STRANGER grabs a chunk of food, and is followed by COBBLER and FRAU CLAAS as the children grapple with the presents.)

FRAU KIERSTED: All night long they feasted. And none of them ate as much as their curious visitor. After dinner, he told them stories of far-away lands. Never once did he say his name or where he had come from. Finally, at the stroke of midnight, he rose from his chair.

STRANGER: I must be away! Thank you very much for a fine dinner and a pleasant Christmas Eve.

(He walks toward left, turns and says:)

STRANGER: Cobbler: don't ever sell that pipe.

FRAU KIERSTED: And a big gust of wind flew down the chimney, and the whole room filled with smoke. Before the family could open their eyes, the stranger was gone.

(FAMILY looks around in disbelief, trying to discover where STRANGER has gone. LIGHTS DIM, STAY DOWN FOR FIVE SECONDS, THEN COME UP; FAMILY is awaking from sleep.)

COBBLER CLAAS: Wife, I had a wonderful dream! I dreamed we had a wonderful Christmas dinner. And there were gifts for the children. And—

(SOUND: KNOCKING ON DOOR FROM STAGE RIGHT; HEER HOMMEL enters from right followed by FOUR SOLDIERS; COBBLER and FRAU CLAAS scramble to their feet.)

HEER HOMMEL: We have come to arrest you, Cobbler!

COBBLER CLAAS: Arrest me? But what for?

HEER HOMMEL: You are a wizard! And a thief!

COBBLER CLAAS: What are you talking about?

FRAU CLAAS: Husband—look around you!

COBBLER CLAAS: Why, the little cottage has disappeared…we are standing in the hall of a great mansion!

FRAU CLAAS: The walls are hung with silk curtains and beautiful paintings…cupboards filled with gold and silver platters.

COBBLER CLAAS: And look out the window!

FRAU CLAAS: What a beautiful garden!

COBBLER CLAAS: And a big pond with dozens of geese!

HEER HOMMEL: And not only that, his chest is filled with gold!

(HEER HOMMEL throws open the top of the bench; gold coins spill out onto the floor.)

HEER HOMMEL: Soldiers, arrest this cobbler! Arrest—

(He stops talking as a pair of invisible hands close his mouth, and he is pulled to and fro; the SOLDIERS, likewise, have their arms jerked behind their back and are pummelled and knocked about.)

FRAU KIERSTED: The burgomaster and his soldiers were grabbed by invisible hands. They were thrashed by unseen arms and paddles and tossed hither and thither about the room until they ran outside and away down the street!

HEER HOMMEL & SOLDIERS: Stop! Ouch! Help! Stop! Ouch! Help!

(HEER HOMMEL and SOLDIERS run offstage left; CLAAS FAMILY point and laugh, run their fingers through coins in chest. LIGHTS OUT CENTER AND LEFT; CLAAS FAMILY freeze; LIGHTS UP RIGHT ON FRAU KIERSTED.)

FRAU KIERSTED: And that was the last anyone in New Amsterdam ever saw of Heer Hommel, the jealous burgomaster.

JAN: What happened to the Cobbler and his family?

ANNEKE: Did they get to keep their new house?

FRAU KIERSTED: Oh, yes, children. The Claas family lived on in their wonderful new home, and they never wanted for food or warmth. But how they came by such good fortune, they never did know.

(SPOTLIGHT ON COBBLER, CENTER STAGE; he stoops and picks up a piece of paper.)

FRAU KIERSTED: The only clue they ever had was a piece of paper the Cobbler found slipped under the front door that Christmas morn. All that it said was:

COBBLER CLAAS: *(reads)* "Don't ever sell that pipe." *(looks at the pipe he holds, laughs)*

(LIGHTS OUT.)

THE END

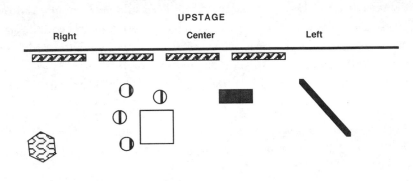

Stage Plan *The Cobbler's Pipe*

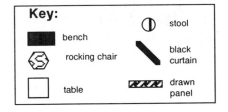

MR. & MRS. CHARLIE T. MULE

Mr. & Mrs. Charlie T. Mule is a tale from the folklore of the Southern Appalachian mountains. A great deal of Appalachian folklore is *didactic*, meaning it is used to teach lessons about everyday life. Folk tales from this part of America aren't so much concerned about kings and queens or warriors and other larger-than-life figures; most of the stories tend to involve ordinary folks—who have extraordinary things happen to them, like the Mules, er, the Pooles.

TIME: Just last week or so

PLACE: A shady mountain hollow in Eastern Kentucky

CAST:

Little Cindy	Bobby
Charlie T. Poole #1	Eddie
Mondie Poole#1	Granny Parker
Charlie T. Poole #2	Doc Thompson
Mondie Poole#2	Preacher Henry
Solomon Shell	8 Square Dancers

STAGE SET: a rock; a half-door; a rocking chair; a hat rack; a desk and chair

PROPS: broom; hat rack; calendar; measuring cup; stethoscope; tongue depressor; fiddle; book

SPECIAL EFFECTS: thunder, lightning sounds; lightning flashes

COSTUMES: early 20th-century rural Appalachian dress—overalls and floppy hats for men, calico dresses and bonnets for women; a mule head; a mule lower torso; monkey tail and mask; large grinning marshmallow head

(LIGHTS UP STAGE RIGHT where a young girl, LITTLE CINDY, sits on a rock reading a book. Two boys, BOBBY and EDDIE, enter from stage left, arguing and pushing, squaring off at center stage.)

BOBBY: Oh, yeh?

EDDIE: Says who?

BOBBY: Says me!

EDDIE: Go on!

BOBBY: Make me!

EDDIE: Make me make you!

(They stop and glower at each other; LITTLE CINDY looks up and coughs.)

LITTLE CINDY: Ahem.

BOBBY: Oh, hi, Little Cindy!

EDDIE: Gosh, we didn't see you sitting there.

LITTLE CINDY: That's because you're both being foolish and rude, Bobby and Eddie.

BOBBY: Says who?

EDDIE: Says her!

LITTLE CINDY: You'd better watch out what you say. Today is an Amber Day, you know.

BOBBY: Amber Day? What's an Amber Day?

LITTLE CINDY: If you make a false wish on an Amber Day, it will come true.

EDDIE: Aw, that's a bunch of hooey! I don't believe it! Do you, Bobby?

BOBBY: Naw! That's just girl stuff! Come on, let's go. *(They exit right.)*

LITTLE CINDY: Those boys can say what they want...but I know different. Down here in Kentucky, you've got to be awful careful what you wish for on an Amber Day. Like those neighbors we had a couple years ago, Mr. and Mrs. Charlie T. Poole. They lived down the hollow a mile or so, and they were just the arguing-est pair of folks you ever did see. *(exits right)*

(LIGHTS DOWN RIGHT, LIGHTS UP CENTER on CHARLIE POOLE and MONDIE POOLE. MONDIE is sweeping the floor, CHARLIE sits in a rocking chair, snoozing; MONDIE tries to sweep around his feet and pokes his feet with her broom, waking him.)

CHARLIE: What in the world? Say, watch what you're doing with that thing!

MONDIE: Charlie Poole, I'm trying to do some work around this place, and your big feet are in the way!

CHARLIE: Well, I'll just get my big feet out of the way, if you'd ever ask politely!

(They glare at each other; MONDIE begins sweeping. CHARLIE gets up, stumbles over the broom, bumps into her and falls down.)

MONDIE: Always in the way! Always bumping and clumping around like an old mule! Why, you're nothing but a mule from the waist down!

CHARLIE: Oh, stop your yammering, woman! The way you're always braying at people, why you're nothing but a mule from the neck up!

(SOUND: THUNDER, LIGHTNING CRACK. LIGHTS GO OUT FOR SEVERAL SECONDS while the actors onstage as MONDIE and CHARLIE exit left and are replaced by another MONDIE (with a mule-head mask) and CHARLIE (with a four-legged mule bottom) who enter stage right. LIGHTS UP ON CENTER STAGE.)

MONDIE: Eee-yaw! Eee-yaw!

CHARLIE: Oh, my goodness! Mondie! What's happened to you?

MONDIE: Eee-yaw! Eee-yaw! *(she points to his legs)*

CHARLIE: No! *(jumps back and tries to run but bumps into chair)*

(They stare at each other, then rush over to a calendar hanging from a hat rack.)

CHARLIE: By golly, Mondie—it's an Amber Day. And we've been turned into mules because of our false wishes!

MONDIE: Eee-yaw! Eee-yaw!

CHARLIE: What are we gonna do?

MONDIE: Eee-yaw! Eee-yaw!

CHARLIE: What? Speak up, I say, speak up, Mondie, can't understand a word you're saying!

MONDIE: Eee-yaw! Eee-yaw! *(stamps her feet)*

CHARLIE: Oh, right. Well, I guess I better go for help.

(SOUND: Knocking on door from stage left. MONDIE and CHARLIE hide behind chair. GRANNY PARKER stands at half door and enters from left, holding a measuring cup, not looking at them as she talks.)

GRANNY PARKER: Howdy, neighbors! It's just Granny Parker from next door. Don't you mind, I'll let myself in. Why, I'm baking an apple pie, and I've come up just a little short on sugar. I was wondering if I could borrow just a pinch? *(GRANNY PARKER looks at MONDIE and CHARLIE and screams.)* Aiii-yeeeee! Oh, my word— the Pooles have become mules! *(She runs offstage left.)*

CHARLIE: Mondie, we've got to do something before they put us in the circus.

MONDIE: Eee-yaw! Eee-yaw!

CHARLIE: Or the zoo! Come on!

(He takes her by the hand, and they cross to upstage left where DOC THOMPSON sits dozing at his desk on other side of half door; MONDIE hides behind CHARLIE.)

CHARLIE: Uh, Doc Thompson?

DOC THOMPSON: *(wakes)* Why, Charlie T. Poole! Come in and sit down.

CHARLIE: Uh, can't come in, Doc. Can't sit down, either.

DOC THOMPSON: *(rises)* What? Well, what's the matter with—oh, great grumbling guinea pigs! Mondie Poole, is that you?

MONDIE: *(shakes her head, stamps her feet)* Eee-yaw! Eee-yaw!

DOC THOMPSON: *(goes around half door)* Well, I guess I'd better examine you two. *(takes stethoscope and holds it against CHARLIE'S chest)* Hmmmmm…*(takes tongue depressor and sticks it in MONDIE'S mouth)* Say "aaaaaahh"…

MONDIE: Eee-yaw! Eee-yaw!

DOC THOMPSON: That's a good girl. Open wide.

CHARLIE: What is it, Doc?

DOC THOMPSON: Well, from the looks of it, I'd say you both have come down with a bad case of…hoof-and-mouth disease. *(laughs)*

CHARLIE: Aw, Doc! That's not funny!

MONDIE: Eee-yaw! Eee-yaw!

DOC THOMPSON: I'm sorry. I couldn't resist. Folks, it's Amber Day, and there's not a thing in the world medical science can do for the kind of situation you've got yourselves into. Come on, let's go see old Solomon Shell, the fiddler.

CHARLIE: A fiddler? Can he cure us?

DOC THOMPSON: Mmmmm, probably not. But he'll make you dance so you forget what ails you!

MONDIE: Eee-yaw! Eee-yaw!

(DOC THOMPSON, CHARLIE and MONDIE walk toward stage right where SOLOMON SHELL sits, playing his fiddle. At center stage they pass PREACHER HENRY, sitting in the rocking chair, reading.)

CHARLIE: Afternoon, Preacher Henry.

PREACHER HENRY: *(looks up, smiles)* Why, hello, Charlie. Mondie. Doc.

MONDIE: Eee-yaw! Eee-yaw!

PREACHER HENRY: *(double takes)* Saints preserve us! It's the end of the world! Men are turning into beasts! *(jumps up, dashes offstage left)*

DOC THOMPSON: He always was a bit fidgety. Come on. Here's Solomon's cabin. Solomon! Solomon Shell, open up, we need your help.

SOLOMON SHELL: (gets up) Well, I will if I can. And I won't if I can't. If it's a fiddle you need, it's a riddle we'll heed.

DOC THOMPSON: Solomon, Mondie and Charlie Poole here have got a problem.

SOLOMON SHELL: Well now! If I could make one whole mule from the two of you, I'd trade my best pig for it. *(walks around them)* Trouble is, there's no neck to connect Mondie's head with Charlie's legs.

MONDIE: Eee-yaw! Eee-yaw!

SOLOMON SHELL: Hold on, I'm doing my best! You know, I've got to play a square dance right now. Maybe the dancing will shake something loose.

(EIGHT SQUARE DANCERS enter from stage left, cross to center stage and form a square. DOC THOMPSON leads CHARLIE and MONDIE in front of dancers, while SOLOMON SHELL fiddles and calls.

SQUARE DANCERS do a basic dance; CHARLIE and MONDIE mime actions in call. Music: Arkansas Traveler.)

SOLOMON SHELL: *(calls)*
>Swing your partner round and round
>Up she goes and then she's down
>Swing her till she turns bright blue
>Pull her hair and yell, "Yahoo!"
>
>Now ladies up and ladies in
>Grab your partner by the chin
>Smack him high and smack him low
>And ride him like a buffalo
>
>And as you romp around the floor
>Tickle him till he begs "No more!"
>Then let him up and spin him clear
>Get on your knees and wiggle your ears
>
>Up on your feet and bow to your man
>Jump in the air as high as you can
>Put your hands behind your back
>Walk like a duck and go "Quack! Quack!"

(SOUND: THUNDER, LIGHTNING CRACK; MUSIC STOPS. LIGHTS GO OUT FOR SEVERAL SECONDS while the actors on-stage as mule MONDIE and mule CHARLIE exit left and are replaced by original MONDIE and CHARLIE who enter stage right. LIGHTS UP ON CENTER STAGE.)

CHARLIE: I can't believe it! We're human again!

DOC THOMPSON: Solomon's square dance calls must have had the right words to end the spell!

(SQUARE DANCERS applaud, cheer, clap SOLOMON on the back.)

SOLOMON: I think it was the fiddling myself.

MONDIE: Oh, thank you, Solomon! Thank you so much! Won't you come have supper with us? We owe you a big favor. Of course, this wouldn't have happened if Charlie hadn't been such an old—

(Charlie and Doc Thompson clap their hands over her mouth.)

SQUARE DANCERS: Sssshhhhhh!

DOC THOMPSON: Now, Mondie—it's just turned eleven o'clock. Amber Day has another hour to run. You be careful what comes out of your mouth.

(CHARLIE leads MONDIE offstage left followed by DOC THOMPSON and four of the SQUARE DANCERS; the other SQUARE DANCERS and SOLOMON SHELL exit right. SPOTLIGHT STAGE RIGHT ON LITTLE CINDY, SITTING ON ROCK.)

LITTLE CINDY: So that was the true story of Mr. and Mrs. Charlie T. Mule. I mean Poole. And it just goes to prove, when Amber Day comes round, you better watch out what you wish for.

BOBBY: *(o.s.)* Oh, yeh? Well, you're a big sappy marshmallow-head!

LITTLE CINDY: Bobby? Eddie?

EDDIE: *(o.s.)* Yeh? Well, you're nothing but a hopping chimpanzee!

LITTLE CINDY: Uh-ohhhhh … *(exits right)*

(BOBBY enters from stage right, EDDIE from stage left; BOBBY has a tail and a monkey mask and hops on all fours; EDDIE has a huge grinning marshmallow head on his shoulders. They meet at center stage, see each other, scream, point and fall down in a faint. LIGHTS OUT.)

THE END

Arkansas Traveler

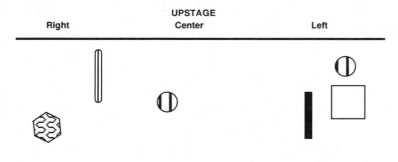

Stage Plan *Mr. & Mrs. Charlie T. Mule*

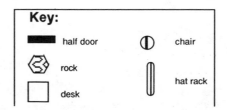

GLUSCABI AND HIS MAGIC GAME BAG

Gluscabi and His Magic Game Bag is based on two Native American stories, one from the Abenaki tribe of Vermont, New Hampshire and southern Quebec, the other from the Cherokee tribe of North Carolina and Oklahoma. In the Abenaki language, Gluscabi means "One Who Tells Stories," and he is the central character in many tales about the creation of the world—a good-hearted superhero who sometimes makes childish mistakes with his powers but does his best to make things right in the end.

TIME: Back when animals talked to people, and people listened

PLACE: In the Eastern Woodlands of North America

CAST:

Father	Rabbit
Son	Squirrel
Gluscabi	Mouse
Grandmother	Woodchuck
Deer	Wildcat
Moose	Fox
Porcupine	Wolf
Bear	Raccoon
5 Hungry People	5 Hunters

STAGE SET: barren with some medium-sized boulders to sit on and lean against (painted styrofoam, cardboard)

PROPS: Father's large bow; Son's small bow; Gluscabi's large bow; 2 large bows for Hunters; 2 spears for Hunters; 1 club or tomahawk for Hunters; large bag; drums; rattles; a game bag (gunny sack)

COSTUMES: all characters can dress in simple one-piece, one-color smocks and sandals; animal masks and headdresses can be made for animal characters; faces of The People and Hunters can be painted with simple designs based on Native American symbols

(LIGHTS UP ON STAGE. At stage right FATHER sits on a rock, stringing a bow; his SON enters from right and approaches him with a small bow.)

SON: Father, when will I be able to join you on the hunt?

FATHER: It will not be long now, my son. You have learned well much of what you will need to provide for your family and your village.

SON: I think I am ready now. Everyone says I am the best shot of any boy in the village.

FATHER: *(chuckles)* There is more to being a good hunter than shooting a bow and arrow. A good hunter must understand the animals he hunts. Understand them and respect them.

SON: Respect them? What do you mean?

FATHER: Sit, and I will tell you a story.

(SON sits at FATHER'S feet; from left, FIVE PEOPLE enter holding drums and rattles, crossing to center stage where they sit in a semicircle facing audience.)

FATHER: Long ago, when the Creator made the world, the first people did not know how to hunt animals. They lived for a time on the bounty of plants and trees, but then they became very hungry.

PERSON #1: Oh, Great Creator, your people are hungry! We are very hungry!

PERSON #2: We thank you for the food you have given us. But we must have more food than what grows from the ground.

PERSON #3: We are cold and without shelter! Please, O Creator, help us!

PERSON #4: Maker of All That Is Good, listen to our request!

PERSON #5: Help us, and we will make new songs for you!

(THE PEOPLE stand and strike up a simple 4/4 beat with instruments that continues for 20-30 seconds; GLUSCABI enters from right with his bow and arrow and dances to center stage. THE PEOPLE stop playing and point at him.)

PEOPLE: It is Gluscabi! He has come to help us!

GLUSCABI: I am Gluscabi, and I am a great hunter!

PEOPLE: Gluscabi is a great hunter!

GLUSCABI: The Creator has heard your sorrow. He has sent me to help you.

PEOPLE: Help us! Help us!

GLUSCABI: I will hunt now. Go now and wait until I return.

(THE PEOPLE whoop and dash offstage left; GLUSCABI crouches and slowly stalks stage with bow and arrow at the ready. A RABBIT and A SQUIRREL enter stealthily from right.)

RABBIT: Squirrel—who is that walking through the woods bent over in such a funny way?

SQUIRREL: I do not know, Rabbit. But he certainly looks funny. Let us see where he goes.

(They crouch and follow behind GLUSCABI, who does not see them; MOUSE, WOODCHUCK and RACCOON enter from left.)

MOUSE: Look. Rabbit and Squirrel are following someone.

WOODCHUCK: They are following Gluscabi. I wonder why?

RACCOON: He looks like he is hunting something. Maybe we should help.

(MOUSE, WOODCHUCK and RACCOON fall in behind RABBIT and SQUIRREL as GLUSCABI continues to crouch and stalk, unaware of their presence. GLUSCABI stops and gazes around him, perplexed.)

GLUSCABI: This is most curious. I have come to hunt game for The People, and all of a sudden, I can find no animals.

(ANIMALS giggle.)

SQUIRREL: Gluscabi may be a great hunter, but he is a few feathers short of a wigwam.

(ANIMALS laugh louder; GLUSCABI peers around, very confused.)

GLUSCABI: I know you animals are in these woods. I hear you laughing. Go ahead and laugh now, my friends, but when I return tomorrow, it is Gluscabi who will be dancing with laughter.

(ANIMALS scurry offstage left, tittering; GRANDMOTHER enters from right, and GLUSCABI stops her at center.)

GLUSCABI: Grandmother! I need your help. I need your help very much.

GRANDMOTHER: A grandmother is always happy to help her grandchild. For that is how the knowledge of the world is best passed down. How can I help you today, Gluscabi?

GLUSCABI: Please, grandmother, make me a game bag.

GRANDMOTHER: A game bag? You are already a great hunter. Why do you need a game bag?

GLUSCABI: A *magic* game bag, Grandmother. So that no matter how much you put into it, there is always room for more.

GRANDMOTHER: That sounds like an interesting idea. I will be happy to make such a bag for you.

(As drums and rattles play offstage, GRANDMOTHER waves her arms for several seconds, turns once around in a circle and draws a game bag out from under her dress; music stops.)

GRANDMOTHER: O Creator, please fill this game bag with wisdom as well as magic.

GLUSCABI: *(takes the bag)* Thank you, Grandmother. Now I will be the greatest hunter of all!

(GRANDMOTHER exits right; GLUSCABI walks around stage with his game bag.)

GLUSCABI: All you animals, listen to me! A terrible thing is about to happen. The sun is going to become dark and die. The world will end, and everything will be destroyed.

(ANIMALS begin to creep onstage: from left—MOUSE, WOOD-CHUCK, RACCOON, RABBIT, SQUIRREL; from right—DEER, WILDCAT, MOOSE, FOX, PORCUPINE, WOLF, BEAR.)

GLUSCABI: Do you hear me, animals? The world is going to end! Come here and save yourselves!

(ANIMALS gather around GLUSCABI at center stage.)

BEAR: Gluscabi, I am a bear and strong as any creature. But I cannot stop the sun from going dark.

WILDCAT: Nor can I, Wildcat, fierce though I be, survive the end of the world. What can we do?

GLUSCABI: My friends, just climb into this magic bag. You will be safe in there when the world is destroyed.

ANIMALS: Ahhhh, yes, yes! We will be safe in the magic bag!

(GLUSCABI goes to the large rock at up left; he holds out the bag to one side and coaxes the ANIMALS to enter; one by one, the ANIMALS climb into it—make entry motions and dart off to the side behind the rock.)

MOOSE: Thank you, Gluscabi. This is most kind. *(enters bag)*

DEER: You are very thoughtful, Gluscabi. *(enters bag)*

FOX: *(starts to enter, then pulls back)* I am not used to being treated so nicely by a hunter, Gluscabi. Why do you want to help us animals?

GLUSCABI: If the world ends, Fox, and there are no animals, what will I hunt?

FOX: *(ponders, shrugs)* I suppose you are right. Catch you on the flip side. *(enters bag)*

GLUSCABI: Come along, Porcupine! You are the last one!

PORCUPINE: I am moving...uh...as fast...uh...as I can. *(squeezes slowly into bag)*

GLUSCABI: Easy with those quills. The bag is not *that* big. *(closes bag and hoists it aloft)* But it *is* big enough to hold every animal in the world! *(laughs)*

(As drums and rattles play offstage, GLUSCABI dances around stage with bag as GRANDMOTHER enters from right; music stops and GLUSCABI stops her at center stage.)

GLUSCABI: Grandmother, look! I put every animal in the world inside the magic game bag you made for me!

GRANDMOTHER: You have worked very hard, my grandson. And what will you do with this bag filled with every animal in the world?

GLUSCABI: I will give this bag to The People. And when The People need food, they can just reach into my magic game bag and pull out whatever they want! Is that not wonderful?

GRANDMOTHER: *(shakes her head and turns away)* Oh, Gluscabi... what am I going to tell your father, the Great Creator?

GLUSCABI: Tell him? Is something wrong, Grandmother?

GRANDMOTHER: Gluscabi, you cannot keep all the animals in the world inside the game bag.

GLUSCABI: Why not?

GRANDMOTHER: If they stay inside the bag, they will get sick. And die. And there will be no animals left for The People or their children. Or their children's children.

GLUSCABI: But what about The People? They are starving!

GRANDMOTHER: The People must learn to hunt for themselves. You must teach them, Gluscabi, because that is how they will grow stronger and wiser. And as The People grow stronger and wiser with hunting, the animals will also grow stronger and wiser in trying to avoid being caught. Then the world will be in the right balance.

(She moves to rock at downstage left and sits, head down as if asleep.)

GLUSCABI: I suppose you are right, Grandmother. And I was wrong also to lie to the animals about the sun going dark and the world ending.

(GLUSCABI picks up bag and opens it; all the ANIMALS come out— emerge from behind rock—as offstage drumming and rattling begin. The ANIMALS cavort around stage for a few seconds as GLUSCABI exits left. FIVE HUNTERS enter from right; they carry bows, spears, clubs and attack ANIMALS. Some ANIMALS fall to floor, others scurry off-stage left. HUNTERS cross to center stage and sit in a semicircle facing audience, making eating motions and shaking weapons, then curling up and sleeping.)

SON: That is a good story, Father. And since Gluscabi taught The People how to hunt, we *have* become strong and wise.

FATHER: Not right away, my son. For after The People learned how to hunt, they became greedy. They began to kill animals when they did not need them for food or clothing or shelter. They began to kill animals for sport. And, once again, Gluscabi had a problem.

GRANDMOTHER: *(awakes, stands, calls)* Gluscabi! Gluscabi, come here at once!

(GLUSCABI dashes in from left.)

GLUSCABI: Yes, Grandmother! What do you want?

GRANDMOTHER: *(awakes, calls)* Gluscabi, you have taught The People to hunt. But you did not teach them how to preserve. They are killing so many animals they do not need that soon, there will be no animals left in the world at all.

GLUSCABI: I cannot stop The People from hunting. They would be hungry again. What can I do?

GRANDMOTHER: You must teach them to hunt the right way. You must teach them to respect the animals they hunt.

GLUSCABI: Respect? How can they respect an animal they are going to kill?

GRANDMOTHER: Whenever a hunter wishes to kill an animal, he must prepare in a special way. They must have a ceremony and ask the spirit of the animal for permission to kill it. After they kill the animal, they must ask the animal spirit for forgiveness. That is how the hunters can respect the animals.

GLUSCABI: You are very wise, Grandmother. I will tell this to the hunters. I will change into the form of a bluejay and whisper your words into their ears while they sleep.

(GRANDMOTHER exits left. GLUSCABI ducks behind large rock up left and re-emerges with wings and a bird mask; drums and rattles sound offstage as he swoops over to sleeping HUNTERS and whispers into their ears. Music stops as GLUSCABI exits left and HUNTERS awake and stand.)

HUNTER #1: I had a very strange dream last night.

HUNTER #2: I had a strange dream, too. About a bluejay.

HUNTER #3: I dreamed a bluejay spoke to me. It had a very familiar voice.

HUNTER #4: I dreamed a bluejay spoke to me and told me to respect the animals we hunt.

HUNTER #5: To ask permission of the animal to hunt it.

HUNTER #1: And ask forgiveness when we kill it.

HUNTER #2: That is a good idea. We could have a special ceremony every time we hunt. With many new songs about hunting and bravery.

HUNTER #3: It sounds like something Gluscabi would think of. But Gluscabi is not a bluejay.

HUNTER #4: Nevermind whose idea it is. It is a good idea, and we should try it.

HUNTER #5: Then let us call The People and begin.

(THE FIVE PEOPLE dance in from left, playing drums and rattles; HUNTERS dance briefly, and PEOPLE and HUNTERS dance off-stage left.)

SON: It is good that The People listened to Gluscabi.

FATHER: And that Gluscabi listened to his Grandmother.

SON: Now I understand that a good hunter must learn more than skill and bravery. He must learn respect.

FATHER: You understand well, my son. You will be a great hunter some-day.

SON: Thank you, father. But I was wondering…

FATHER: Yes, my son?

SON: What would happen if there ever came a time when hunters did not respect the animals?

FATHER: If they became greedy and killed not for what they needed?

SON: But only for sport?

FATHER: *(stands)* If that were to happen in this world again, it is said that the sun would truly go dark in the sky.

SON: Would not Gluscabi return with his magic game bag?

FATHER: Gluscabi would return.

SON: And all the animals and people in the world would disappear into his magic game bag?

FATHER: Only this time, they would never escape.

(Drums and rattles play offstage; LIGHTS OUT.)

THE END

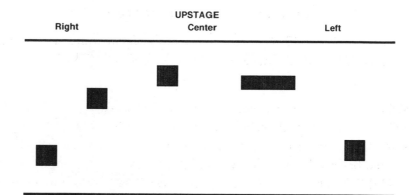

Stage Plan *Gluscabi & His Magic Game Bag*

Key:

rock

THE BEGGAR IN
THE BLANKET

Since the mid-1970s over six hundred thousand persons of Vietnamese descent have emigrated to the United States, bringing with them their ancient folktale traditions and further enriching the already diverse mosaic of contemporary American folklore. *The Beggar in the Blanket* is from the Vietnamese genre of wise man-foolish man tales. In this case, the wise man is actually a woman—Mrs. Kim—who creates a temporary deception to teach her husband the true value of friendship and the importance of family loyalty.

TIME: Many hundreds of years ago

PLACE: A village in the jungle

CAST:
Narrator	Nguyen
Kim	Ton
De	Cao
Mrs. Kim	Duc
Mandarin	Executioner
3 Messengers	4 Servants

STAGE SET: a low table and four floor cushions

PROPS: jewels and coins; a money box; a bowl of noodles; a sword; a rolled-up blanket; sticks and stones; a tinwhistle or recorder or flute; a gong or bell or chime

COSTUMES: all male characters except Mandarin and Executioner can dress in simple tunics and sandals; Mandarin should be more richly dressed and Executioner could wear face mask or hood; Mrs. Kim and any other female should wear the traditional Vietnamese *ao dai* style of women's pant dress

(LIGHTS UP STAGE RIGHT, where Narrator sits on a cushion. He stands, solemnly strikes a gong (bell or chime) and bows to the audience before speaking:)

NARRATOR: Many, many hundreds of years ago in the middle of a deep, deep jungle, there was a tiny village. In the village lived two brothers—Kim and De.

(LIGHTS UP STAGE CENTER on KIM, who sits at table and takes jewels and coins from a money box, counting them gleefully.)

NARRATOR: Kim was the elder brother. He had been a hard worker all of his life, and now he was one of the richest men in the village. He also had the good fortune to have married a woman who was very wise and kind—as well as an excellent cook.

(MRS. KIM enters from left carrying a bowl of noodles that she sets down in front of her husband, who beams with delight; he pulls out chopsticks and begins eating. LIGHTS UP STAGE LEFT on DE, who sits on cushion; he fools with a sandal strap, then puts it down and picks up a tinwhistle or recorder.)

NARRATOR: The younger brother, De, was not such a hard worker. Even though he was a very good shoemaker, he only worked when he needed something to eat, and he never worked for very long. De lived alone because he could not afford to feed a wife. But he was happy because he loved to play the flute and make up songs and poems.

(De plays a few notes on tinwhistle.)

DE: I sing today of sunrise that decorates the dawn; the cloud that travels through the morning sky is as pretty as a swan.

(DE plays a few notes on tinwhistle, then rests. LIGHTS DOWN ON STAGE LEFT. At center stage, MRS. KIM stands next to her husband.)

MRS. KIM: Husband?
KIM: Yes, my jewel?
MRS. KIM: You have been very busy working these past few months.
KIM: Oh, yes, yes! Work is good! Work brings money! And money is very good! *(laughs)*

MRS. KIM: When did you last see your brother, De?

KIM: My brother? *(snorts)* Why, I don't know. I have been too busy working to think about that sluggard!

MRS. KIM: Perhaps you should invite him to have dinner with us some night. You know how you love to hear him play his flute.

KIM: *(stands)* Dinner? That is impossible! What would all my rich friends think if they came to our house and found that lazy brother of mine sitting at our table? *(slams fist on table)* They would be insulted! They would think I had lost my mind! They would never come to my house again.

MRS. KIM: Maybe that would not be so bad. After all, husband—friends are not the same as a brother.

KIM: And it is a very good thing they are not! If my friends were as lazy as my brother, the entire village would starve!

(KIM exits right; MRS. KIM sits at table, hands folded, pondering.)

NARRATOR: Mrs. Kim saw that arguing with her stubborn husband was of no use. Just the same, she decided she would make him come to understand the true value of a brother, even a poor and lazy brother like De.

(NARRATOR strikes gong; LIGHTS OUT, THEN UP AGAIN. A rolled-up blanket is on the floor behind the table and to the left. MRS. KIM sits at table, her head down; she is crying. KIM enters from right, striding purposefully; he sees her distress and rushes to her.)

KIM: My wife! My jewel! What is the matter? Why are you crying?

MRS. KIM: Oh, husband, a terrible thing has happened! A most terrible, terrible thing!

KIM: What has happened? Tell me at once!

MRS. KIM: While you were away last night, a beggar man came to our door.

KIM: A beggar? To our door?

MRS. KIM: *(stands)* He tried to rob us. I chased him with my broomstick, and he started to ran away. But then he tripped over a log and fell—right there on the hearthstone. He hit his head on the stone...

KIM: And?

MRS. KIM: He died. *(covers her eyes, cries)*

KIM: Wife, that is indeed terrible. Where is the body?

MRS. KIM: *(points to blanket)* There in the corner. I wrapped him in that old blanket. Oh, husband, it was not my fault he died. You must believe me!

KIM: I do believe you. But the Mandarin—

MRS. KIM: The Mandarin will think I murdered a helpless old beggar. I will be sent to jail and you will be fined a great deal of money. We are ruined!

(She sits at table, weeps; KIM paces in front of table.)

KIM: There must be something we can do. There must be. There absolutely must be. *(stops pacing)* But I cannot think of it. I will have to go before the mandarin and confess that my wife has killed a beggar. Oh, the humiliation! My friends will never speak to me again!

MRS. KIM: Husband?

KIM: Yes?

MRS. KIM: I have an idea. If you can get one of your friends to help you, you can carry the blanket into the jungle and bury the beggar. No one will miss a poor old beggar.

KIM: Wife, that is an excellent idea. You are a very wise woman. I will go see my good friend Nguyen at once.

(MRS. KIM bows her head; KIM rushes out and goes to the cushion upstage right where NGUYEN, who enters from right, sits with head bowed.)

KIM: Nguyen!

NGUYEN: *(looks up)* Kim! My good friend Kim! How are you today?

KIM: Not so good. While I was away last night, a beggar tried to rob our house.

NGUYEN: What terrible news, my good friend!

KIM: There is worse. My wife surprised him, and he fell on the hearthstone trying to run away.

NGUYEN: Good for her! Serves that cowardly thief right!

KIM: But the beggar struck his head and died. I need your help to move his body to the jungle and bury him before anyone finds out what has happened.

NGUYEN: That is a very good plan, my good friend Kim. A very good plan.

KIM: Then you will help me bury the beggar?

NGUYEN: I would *like* to help you. But I am old and weak. I would be of no help at all. Why don't you go across the road and ask Ton?

KIM: Ton? Yes, that is an excellent idea. He is a good friend, too. Thank you for your advice.

NGUYEN: Anytime!

(KIM runs across stage to cushion upstage left where TON, who enters from left, sits with head bowed.)

KIM: Ton! I need your help!

TON: My good friend Kim! It is wonderful to see you. How may I be of service today?

KIM: While I was away last night, a beggar tried to rob our house. My wife surprised him, and he fell on the hearthstone trying to run away.

TON: You were very lucky.

KIM: Unfortunately, he struck his head and died. I need your help to move his body to the jungle and bury him before anyone finds out.

TON: *(squirms, grimaces)* Ohhhhh....

KIM: What is wrong!

TON: *(clutches stomach, moans)* My stomach! I have had terrible pains all morning! Ohhhhhh...

KIM: But I need your help to bury the beggar!

TON: Oh, I would be happy to help you any other time. But I am so sick! I could not carry anything! Ohhhhhh...*(falls over, moans)*

KIM: Well then...I will see my good friend Cao. Surely he will be able to help me.

(KIM runs across stage to cushion upstage right where CAO, who enters from right, sits with head bowed.)

KIM: Good friend Cao! I need your help today!

CAO: Welcome, good friend Kim! Would you like a cup of tea?

KIM: I have no time for tea. My wife has accidentally killed a beggar who tried to rob us, and I need your help to bury his body in the jungle.

CAO: *(stands)* Oh, good friend Kim...I just remembered. I have to go to the next village and visit my wife's family. It is my mother-in-law's birthday, and she will be very angry if I do not come. Goodbye, good friend Kim! *(bows, rushes off right)*

(KIM runs across stage to cushion upstage left where DUC, who enters from left, sits with head bowed.)

KIM: Good friend Duc! I need your help right away!

DUC: Help you? Oh, I could not possibly help you this evening. My wife is very ill. I do not want to leave her alone in the house. Not with all these nasty beggars roaming around. Why, what if one tried to come in my house and rob us?

(DUC bows his head; KIM stands silent for a few moments, then walks slowly back to center stage and his wife sitting at the table.)

KIM: My jewel, none of my friends can help me!

MRS. KIM: Fine friends you have, husband! They come to your house and eat your food and drink your tea, but when you need their help—where are they? It's a lucky thing you have a brother. Go get De to help you bury the blanket.

KIM: De? Why would he want to help me? *(hangs head)* I...I have never done anything for him.

MRS. KIM: That is true. But he *is* your brother. If he will not help you in your time of need, no one will. *(she exits right)*

(KIM hesitates, then scurries across stage to cushion upstage left where DE sits, playing with his flute.)

DE: Brother! It is so good to see you! How are you?

KIM: It is good to see you, too. Brother...I need your help. Last night a beggar robbing our house fell and killed himself. I am afraid my wife will be charged with his murder. I need someone to help me bury the beggar's body.

DE: *(embraces Kim)* Brother, I will help you.

(NARRATOR strikes gong; LIGHTS OUT, THEN UP AGAIN. MRS. KIM sits at table, KIM and DE sit on floor on either side of table. THREE MESSENGERS enter from right and cross to center.)

MESSENGER #1: You three—come with us immediately!

MESSENGER #2: You have been summoned to appear before the Royal Mandarin!

MESSENGER #3: Make haste! The Mandarin must not be kept waiting!

(NARRATOR strikes gong and MANDARIN enters from left with FOUR SERVANTS trailing behind; an EXECUTIONER bearing a sword follows the SERVANTS. MESSENGERS and SERVANTS group themselves behind the table; KIM, MRS. KIM and DE bow to MANDARIN and kneel before him.)

KIM: Your lordship, to what do we owe the honor of your visit to our humble home?

MANDARIN: Your wife murdered a helpless old beggar. Last night you went to the homes of four honest men and tried to persuade them to help you bury the beggar's body.

(NGUYEN and CAO enter from right, TON and DUC from left and point accusing fingers at KIM.)

MANDARIN: These men followed you into the jungle and watched you bury the body under a tree. Then they dug up the body and brought it here to me.

KIM: My friends? How could you betray me?

MANDARIN: They were only doing their duty. As will my executioner do his before this day has ended.

(EXECUTIONER steps forward, flexes sword, bows, steps back into place.)

KIM: But your lordship, my wife did not murder the beggar—

MANDARIN: Silence! We have proof! Servants, bring the blanket!

(FOUR SERVANTS bring the rolled-up blanket to center stage.)

MANDARIN: Servants, unroll the blanket!

(SERVANTS unroll the blanket; everyone shouts with surprise as blanket reveals no body—only sticks and stones. KIM and DE rise, but MRS. KIM stays kneeling.)

NGUYEN: The body is gone!

TON: We saw Kim and De bury it!

CAO: In the jungle, in the middle of the night!

MANDARIN: Nguyen, Ton, Cao, Duc! You each swore this man and his wife had killed a helpless beggar. You claimed a reward! Where is the beggar!

DUC: Maybe a tiger dug it up and ran away with it.

MANDARIN: Silence! Executioner, come forward!

(EXECUTIONER steps forward, brandishing sword.)

MANDARIN: Add these four to your list of villagers receiving haircuts today!

(MRS. KIM rises, steps up to MANDARIN.)

MRS. KIM: Your lordship, wait! There is no beggar.

KIM & DE: No beggar?

NGUYEN, TON, CAO & DUC: No beggar?

MESSENGERS & SERVANTS: No beggar?

MANDARIN: Would you repeat what you just said?

MRS. KIM: There is no beggar. I made up the story to show my husband that the love of his brother was more valuable than the love of his rich, so-called friends—the friends who not only refused to help him, but betrayed him for a base reward.

(NGUYEN, TON, CAO and DUC hang heads, turn away in shame.)

MANDARIN: You, Mrs. Kim, are a very clever woman. I am greatly impressed by your wisdom. And by the kindness you have shown to your husband's brother. I hope, Kim, that you have learned a lesson from this.

KIM: I have, your lordship. I have learned that the love of my family is the most precious of all my possessions.

DE: And I have learned that I should never help my brother bury some-one—unless he actually has a body to bury!

(Everyone laughs; NARRATOR strikes gong and everyone freezes. LIGHTS OUT.)

THE END

Kim/Mrs. Kim

Nguyen/Cao

De/Ton/Duc

Narrator

Stage Plan *The Beggar in the Blanket*

Key:

☐ table   ◖ cushion

PATCHES SOLVES A WEDDING RIDDLE

Patches Solves a Wedding Riddle comes from the folklore of African-Americans living on the Sea Isles, a group of islands off the coast of Georgia and South Carolina. The people who settled these islands in the early 18th century developed a unique dialect called Gullah—a combination of English and African words and grammar drawn from several West African languages, including Hausa, Ibo, Ewe, Mende, Twi and Yoruba—and several words of Gullah origin have entered modern English, including *goober, jukebox, tote, banjo, okra* and *yam*. The famous Bre'r Rabbit-Uncle Remus stories were originally recited in Gullah, and Gullah tales often use riddles, recited in verse or sing-song melodies that emphasize the melodic flow of the dialect's speech pattern.

TIME: Late-1800s

PLACE: Coast of Georgia

CAST: Narrator   Governor
          Patches   Governor's Wife
          Patches' Mother   Governor's Daughter
          Suitor   3 Riddle Police Chiefs
          3 Maids

STAGE SET: tree stump; swamp scrim

PROPS: harmonica; bag of groceries; stool; paper fan; parasol

COSTUMES: 19th-century Southern rural dress for Narrator and Patches' Mother; Governor should wear top hat and fancy frock coat; Governor's Wife and Governor's Daughter can dress in ballroom gowns with hoop skirts; Maids can wear frilly dresses; Riddle Police Chiefs might appear in Keystone Cop outfits with ? marks on their helmets; Suitor can be dressed as a well-to-do dandy; Patches could wear a raggedy flannel shirt and ragged overalls with knee patches, battered cap or hat

(LIGHTS UP FULL; at stage right NARRATOR sits on a tree stump, playing a harmonica. He stops playing and greets the audience:)

NARRATOR: Hello, y'all! Let me quizzit you. Anybody here like riddles? Well, once upon a time down South around Georgia, where I come from, the governor and his wife had a pretty daughter with the most beautiful *ye-yes*—that's eyes. And they all liked to tell riddles from dayclean to nightfresh, just as many riddles as they could squeeze in a day.

(GOVERNOR enters from left followed by GOVERNOR'S WIFE followed by DAUGHTER; they gather in a circle at center stage.)

DAUGHTER: Riddle me rye, riddle me ree! Can you guess this riddle from me?

GOVERNOR'S WIFE: Riddle us prompt, riddle us quick—

GOVERNOR: Riddle us while the clock does tick!

DAUGHTER: *(holds out her hand)* Four fingers and a thumb, yet flesh and bone I have none?

GOVERNOR: Ohhhh, let's see now…what could that be?

GOVERNOR'S WIFE: Perhaps the branches of a tree?

DAUGHTER: *(pulls out a glove)* A glove, a glove, my parents kind! Now see if you can riddle as fine!

(GOVERNOR, GOVERNOR'S WIFE and DAUGHTER laugh and skip offstage left, arm-in-arm.)

NARRATOR: They liked to speak in rhymes, too. In fact, these folks were so stirred-up crazy about riddles and rhymes that, when it came about for the daughter to get married, the Governor and his wife decided that the man who could answer the daughter's riddle would gain her hand and a fortune in gold. However, anybody who couldn't guess the riddle…got sent to pull weeds in the swamp—with the alligators.

(An old woman (PATCHES' MOTHER) walks slowly onstage from right, followed by a young boy (PATCHES) carrying a bag of groceries.)

NARRATOR: Well, somewhere around Savannah, there lived an old widow woman and her young son, Patches. That was what everybody called him, on account of all his clothes had been made from different bits of other clothes. Oh, Patches and his mother were awfully poor, but Patches was awfully smart and could sweetmouth anybody. One day he says to his mama:

PATCHES: *(puts down bag)* Mama, I am going to go to Atlanta and guess the Governor's Daughter's riddle! Then I am going to marry her!

PATCHES' MOTHER: Oh, Patches, don't go! Fifty-five men have gone to guess that riddle, and fifty-five men have been fed to the alligators because they couldn't.

PATCHES: I am not going to get eaten, mama! I am going to make us rich!

PATCHES' MOTHER: *(kneels)* You'll just make yourself dead! Please, Patches, don't go! I didn't raise my son to be lunch for a gator!

(SOUND CUE: NARRATOR plays harmonica as PATCHES gives his mother the bag of groceries, shakes her hand and walks toward center stage; PATCHES' MOTHER hesitates a moment, shaking her head, then exits right. A SUITOR, finely dressed, dashes onstage from left, bumping into PATCHES.)

PATCHES: My good sir! I didn't mean to—

SUITOR: Get away! Get away! Save yourself! Run for your life!

PATCHES: Get away from what?

SUITOR: *(pointing behind him toward left)* They've got alligators! Big alligators! Huge alligators! Gigantic alligators! Alligators with teeth this big! *(spreads arms out to full width)*

PATCHES: You must be a suitor come to answer the Governor's Daughter's riddle.

SUITOR: Me? A suitor? Don't be ridiculous! Riddle? What riddle? Ha-ha-ha! You must be mad! I don't know anything about riddles! Really, I don't! Nothing! *(falls to knees, grabs PATCHES' hands)* Please don't let them feed me to the alligators! *(sobs)*

PATCHES: I won't. Because I am going to answer the riddle.

SUITOR: You? *(rises, regards PATCHES with condescension)* You, an obvious country bumpkin dressed like a silly scarecrow? You have come to answer the Governor's Daughter's riddle?

PATCHES: I have. And I will.

SUITOR: You're mad! *(runs offstage right, shouts)* Gator bait!

PATCHES: Strange fellow. *(shrugs)* I suppose the Governor's House is this way.

(PATCHES turns to walk toward left, when the GOVERNOR and GOVERNOR'S WIFE enter from left. They cross to center stage, chatting between themselves, oblivious to PATCHES.)

PATCHES: *(bowing)* Excuse me, but could you tell me where I might find the Governor and his wife?

(They stop talking and look at him curiously, circling around him.)

GOVERNOR: And why would you be seeking they?

GOVERNOR'S WIFE: Surely, he has lost his way.

PATCHES: Nosir, mister; nosir, ma'am. I've come to gain their daughter's hand.

GOVERNOR: My boy, you can't be serious at all!

GOVERNOR'S WIFE: The lad is deluded. Give the sheriff a call!

PATCHES: I'm not deluded; my brain is sound. Just tell me where they can be found.

GOVERNOR: I am the Governor—

GOVERNOR'S WIFE: And *I* the Governor's Wife.

GOVERNOR: Are you ready to risk *your* life?

GOVERNOR'S WIFE: If you miss the riddle—

GOVERNOR: There's no second chance.

PATCHES: Well then, I'll see you all at the Wedding Dance!

GOVERNOR: First, you must prove you are worthy of this test.

GOVERNOR'S WIFE: Otherwise, you waste our time in jest. Bring in the Chiefs of the Riddle Police!

(THREE RIDDLE POLICE CHIEFS enter from right; they stand in a line and face PATCHES, the GOVERNOR and GOVERNOR'S WIFE flank PATCHES' opposite side.)

RIDDLE POLICE CHIEF #1: Tell me, what is red and blue and purple and green? No one can reach it, not even a queen?

PATCHES: A rainbow in the sky, the last I've seen!

RIDDLE POLICE CHIEF #2: What flies forever, rests never and is never caught?

PATCHES: The wind, the wind, or so I've always thought.

RIDDLE POLICE CHIEF #3: What was born when the world was made, but older than a month never grows?

PATCHES: The moon up above—why, look how it glows!

RIDDLE POLICE CHIEF #1: And how much, how much is the moon above worth?

PATCHES: A dollar—it has four quarters, of that I'm sure.

RIDDLE POLICE CHIEF #2: Tell me, young man, what has a heart in its head?

PATCHES: You must mean lettuce—green, purple or red.

RIDDLE POLICE CHIEF #3: Then, what has a head but not any hair?

PATCHES: A pin or a nail—have you some to spare?

RIDDLE POLICE CHIEF #1: What has a head but cannot think?

PATCHES: A match laying on the kitchen sink.

RIDDLE POLICE CHIEF #2: What has plenty teeth but cannot eat?

PATCHES: A comb or a saw—tell me, is their daughter really sweet?

RIDDLE POLICE CHIEF #3: What has legs but can't walk from here to there?

PATCHES: A bed, a table—and most likely a chair.

RIDDLE POLICE CHIEF #1: What passes through a door but never goes in and never comes out?

PATCHES: Must be a keyhole you're speaking about.

RIDDLE POLICE CHIEF #2: Governor, this boy is sharp as steel!

RIDDLE POLICE CHIEF #3: Maybe it's time to let him riddle for real?

GOVERNOR: Very well, send in my daughter dear; she'll decide what happens from here.

(CHIEFS retreat behind GOVERNOR and GOVERNOR'S WIFE as DAUGHTER enters from left with THREE MAIDS: MAID #1 carries a stool, MAID #2 carries a paper fan, MAID #3 carries a parasol; the MAIDS sit DAUGHTER down at center stage, fan her and hold parasol over her head.)

DAUGHTER: So this is my suitor for today? I thought he'd be dressed a bit more gay!

GOVERNOR'S WIFE: Don't let his simple rags deceive; he's a first-class riddler, you better believe!

DAUGHTER: Then tell me, suitor, the answer to this riddle I pose.

PATCHES: When I do, you'll quit laughing at my clothes.

(DAUGHTER shoos away her MAIDS, rises and addresses audience:)

DAUGHTER:
> There were twelve apples hanging high
> When twelve kings came riding past
> Each, he took an apple and walked away from there
> How many were left hanging last?

PATCHES: Now, lady, fairest lady, is that all your riddle there be? Why, I can solve that riddle—sure as you-all looking at me!

DAUGHTER: Then do, please do, tell us true; tell us now without delay.

PATCHES: The answer is eleven, my lady love; what more is there to say?

GOVERNOR: Eleven? Eleven? How can that be—

GOVERNOR'S WIFE: When twelve bold kings—no more, no less— rode underneath that tree?

PATCHES: And the kings rode by, taking none, not one apple taken by they. But the man named Each, he walked by and picked the only apple that day.

DAUGHTER: *(takes PATCHES by the arm)* Mama and daddy, my riddle he's guessed. This is truly the man for me!

GOVERNOR: He's clever and bold—

GOVERNOR'S WIFE: So give him the gold!

DAUGHTER: And we'll live forever and ever—

PATCHES: Happily!

(Arm-in-arm, PATCHES and the GOVERNOR'S DAUGHTER stroll offstage left followed by GOVERNOR and GOVERNOR'S WIFE as CHIEFS and MAIDS chant:)

CHIEFS & MAIDS:
> He solved the wedding riddle, hip-hip hooray! Hip-hip hooray!
> Hip-hip hooray! He solved the wedding riddle, hip-hip hooray!
> Hip-hip hooray, Mister Patches!

(CHIEFS and MAIDS exit left, repeating above chant at lower volume.)

NARRATOR: And that's how a poor boy named Patches married the girl of his dreams. At least he didn't get eaten by gators, it seems. Oh no! Good gosh, good golly, hey-hey! Now, they've even got me talking that way!

(SOUND CUE: NARRATOR blows a final riff on harmonica, then bows. LIGHTS OUT.)

THE END

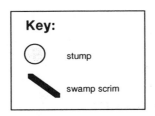

UPSTAGE

Right   Center   Left

Stage Plan *Patches Solves a Wedding Riddle*

Key:

◯   stump

▬   swamp scrim

MAGNUS FOURPENNY AND THE BLACK BEAR BIRTHDAY BASH

Magnus Fourpenny and the Black Bear Birthday Bash is a tale from the Big Thicket region of Southeastern Texas just northeast of Houston and the Gulf of Mexico. Forty miles long and twenty miles wide, the Big Thicket is one of the densest swamp and forest preserves in North America and contains the greatest variety of plants and wild animals of any comparable area on the continent. Hunting is a prime recreational activity in the Big Thicket, and there are many tales about great hunters and famous hunting expeditions. While most hunting tales boast about how big the catch was, *Magnus Fourpenny and the Black Bear Birthday Bash* tells the story of a hunter who came home with empty hands—but a heart full of new-found empathy for his prey.

TIME: About 1920

PLACE: Big Thicket region of Texas

CAST:
Magnus Fourpenny	Buddy Black Bear
Ruby Fourpenny	Bertha Black Bear
3 Fourpenny Children	3 Black Bear Cubs
Aunt Minnie	Aunt Betty Black Bear
Uncle Owen	Uncle Buck Black Bear
Old Dog Sam	

STAGE SET: kitchen table and two chairs; rocks; forest scrim

PROPS: jaw's harp; doll; jacks; basket of clothes; broom and dustpan; shotgun; Magnus' hunting hat; frying pan; shovel; rake; hoe

COSTUMES: rural dress for all human characters—overalls and floppy hats for men, calico dresses and bonnets for women; animals can be in animal masks and costumes

(LIGHTS UP FULL; at right MAGNUS FOURPENNY sits at a table, playing a jaw's harp. The THREE FOURPENNY CHILDREN are on the floor at his feet, playing with a doll and pitching jacks. Magnus' wife, RUBY FOURPENNY, enters from stage left carrying a basket of clothes; a few feet from the table, she halts, sets the basket on the floor, puts her hands on hips and bellows in tones of a drill sergeant)

RUBY FOURPENNY: Maaaaaag-*nusssssss!*

(MAGNUS and CHILDREN are startled and jump away from her.)

MAGNUS FOURPENNY: Hello, darlin'. I mean, honey-bunch. Sweetie-pie!

RUBY FOURPENNY: Magnus Fourpenny, what in the world are you doing?

MAGNUS FOURPENNY: Well, I was just getting ready to give the kids their daily music lesson.

CHILD #1: Yes, momma! Poppa's going to teach us the jaw's harp!

CHILD #2: And we can form a marching band!

CHILD #3: And march all the way to Austin for the Texas Independence Day parade!

RUBY FOURPENNY: Music lessons! Marching bands! Parades! Why, I never heard such foolishness! You should be out earning a living, Magnus Fourpenny! Your nose to the grindstone! Shoulder to the wheel! Putting food on your family's table! But, oh no, not Mister Magnus Fourpenny of Pigeon Roost, Texas—while his devoted wife slaves away, he's got a piece ofbent-up wire stuck between his lips going "boo-biddy-boo-biddy-boo"!

CHILDREN: *(dejectedly)* Mom-ma!

RUBY FOURPENNY: And you children need to be at your chores! Go on, get to it!

CHILDREN: *(dejectedly)* Pop-pa!

MAGNUS FOURPENNY: Better do as momma says, children.

CHILDREN: *(dejectedly)* O-kay!

(CHILDREN pick up toys and exit left; AUNT MINNIE and UNCLE OWEN enter from left. They halt a few feet from table and AUNT MINNIE puts her hands on hips and yells as if calling a hog:)

AUNT MINNIE: Howwwwww-*dyyyyyy!*

MAGNUS FOURPENNY: Well, if it isn't Aunt Minnie and Uncle Owen! Come in and set a spell!

UNCLE OWEN: That's right kind, Magnus. Don't mind if we do.

(MAGNUS gets up and offers chair to AUNT MINNIE who sits; UNCLE OWEN sits in the other chair.)

RUBY FOURPENNY: I suppose you've come to borrow something. Well, whatever it is, we don't have any!

AUNT MINNIE: Why, Ruby Fourpenny, you're as ornery as a mule in a mud puddle! We've walked halfway through the entire Big Thicket just to visit and pass the time of day with you folks.

(RUBY gives a broom to AUNT MINNIE and a dustpan to UNCLE OWEN.)

RUBY FOURPENNY: If you're going to pass time in this house, you might as well be useful. Maybe you can talk my husband into hunting us some supper.

UNCLE OWEN: Are you going hunting, Magnus? They say there's a whole passel of black bear down by Gumstick Pond. Why, they're running thick as briars on a brush pig!

MAGNUS FOURPENNY: Welllllll—

RUBY FOURPENNY: Magnus hunt? Why, he'd rather sit on a stump and watch the snails whiz by.

AUNT MINNIE: Now, Ruby, that's no way to talk to your husband. Remember, honey catches more flies than vinegar.

RUBY FOURPENNY: And flies is all we'll have for supper tonight, if Magnus won't get up and hunt something besides his afternoon nap!

MAGNUS FOURPENNY: Ruby, you can't judge a horse by its harness. I'm going to go hunt us a black bear. When I come back, you'll be happy as a clam in high water.

(RUBY shuffles AUNT MINNIE and UNCLE OWEN offstage right, then exits right herself, glaring at MAGNUS who is busy loading his shotgun and picking up his hunting hat. Offstage, the FOURPENNY CHILDREN sing to melody of Twinkle, Twinkle Little Star:*)*

CHILDREN: *(sing)*
>Poppa, Poppa hunting bear
>Off he goes he knows not where
>Tracking high and tracking low
>In the wind and rain and snow

MAGNUS FOURPENNY: Now, where is that hunting dog of mine? Old Dog Sam! Come on out here now!

(OLD DOG SAM waddles out from right; he is large and slow and silly-looking.)

OLD DOG SAM: Arooo! Arooo! Arf-arf arooo!

MAGNUS FOURPENNY: There you are! Come on, let's get us a bear!

(MAGNUS and SAM stalk around the stage as CHILDREN sing off-stage:)

CHILDREN: *(sing)*
>If he saw a bear today
>He would run the other way
>Poppa, Poppa hunting bear
>Lost out in the woods somewhere

(At down left, MAGNUS motions for SAM to stop.)

MAGNUS FOURPENNY: Tarnation! We've been out in this wilderness all day and all night, and we haven't seen sign of one single solitary bear.

OLD DOG SAM: Arooo! Arooo! Arf-arf arooo!

MAGNUS FOURPENNY: Now, Sam, you're a tracking dog, and all you've been doing since we left home is following me! We're not hunting me; we're hunting bear!

OLD DOG SAM: Arooo! Arooo! Arf-arf arooo!

(A large BLACK BEAR [BUDDY] enters from left behind MAGNUS and SAM; they do not see him.)

MAGNUS FOURPENNY: Hold on!

(MAGNUS kneels and sniffs the ground in front of him; SAM does the same, as the bear cranes to look over their shoulders.)

MAGNUS FOURPENNY: Sam, I smell bear!

OLD DOG SAM: Arooo! Arooo! Arf-arf arooo!

MAGNUS FOURPENNY: From the size of these tracks, I'd say it's a big one.

OLD DOG SAM: Arooo! Arooo! Arf-arf arooo!

MAGNUS FOURPENNY: *(sniffs the air)* And from the smell, I'd say he could use a bath.

OLD DOG SAM: Arooo! Arooo! Arf-arf arooo!

MAGNUS FOURPENNY: I'd estimate he was here an hour ago. Maybe two.

OLD DOG SAM: Arooo! Arooo! Arf-arf arooo!

MAGNUS FOURPENNY: If we hurry, we can catch him by nightfall. Looks like he went thataway! *(points to right)*

(MAGNUS and SAM head right and get almost to end of stage when the Bear, still at left, lets out a roar.)

BUDDY BLACK BEAR: Rrrrrrr-owwwwrrr!

(MAGNUS and SAM turn and stare at BEAR who gives them a little wave of his paw.)

MAGNUS FOURPENNY: It's a bear! Ohmygosh, it's a bear!

OLD DOG SAM: Woof-woof-woof! Woof-woof-woof! Woof-woof-woof!

MAGNUS FOURPENNY: Go on, dog! Get him! Get him, I say!

(BEAR runs to tree and disappears behind it, as MAGNUS raises shotgun, lowers shotgun, urges a reluctant SAM to chase BEAR. SAM runs around in circle chasing his tail, lowers head between paws, whines.)

MAGNUS FOURPENNY: Well, there he went into that big old tree trunk. Sam, you might as well go home. No use the two of us getting eaten.

OLD DOG SAM: Arooo! Arooo! Arf-arf arooo!

MAGNUS FOURPENNY: I know, I know, old friend. But I can't go home and face Ruby and not have a bearskin to show. I'd rather be the main course at a bear brunch than listen to one more second of her scolding. Go on! Go on home now!

(SAM slowly slinks offstage right, whimpering; MAGNUS squares his shoulders and peers into tree.)

MAGNUS FOURPENNY: My hand to heaven, it's as dark as a stack of black cats in there. Look out, brother bear! I'm a-comin' in!

(MAGNUS goes around tree; LIGHTS OUT BRIEFLY, THEN UP AGAIN. BUDDY BLACK BEAR, BERTHA BLACK BEAR and THREE BLACK BEAR CUBS sit on and in front of rocks at up left as MAGNUS enters their den, shotgun raised.)

MAGNUS FOURPENNY: Why, it's an entire tribe of bears!

BERTHA BLACK BEAR: Goodness mercy, didn't you ever learn to knock when entering someone's home?

BUDDY BLACK BEAR: "Tribe"? Bertha, did he say "tribe"? That's such a disorganized word, such a human word. So untidy. What does he take us for?

BERTHA BLACK BEAR: Now, Buddy, he's only human.

BEAR CUB #1: Poppa, do we look like humans?

BEAR CUB #2: Maybe he lost his glasses in the swamp, and he thinks we're humans.

BEAR CUB #3: I'm not sure he thinks much at all. Look at that silly hat.

MAGNUS FOURPENNY: Hold on or I'll shoot! I mean it!

BUDDY BLACK BEAR: Put that thing down before you hurt yourself. Can't you see we're in the middle of a major family function?

BEAR CUB #1: It's my birthday!

BEAR CUB #2: Mine, too!

BEAR CUB #3: And mine! We're all one year old!

BEAR CUB #1: Where's my present?

BEAR CUB #2: Did you bring some honey?

BEAR CUB #3: I want a honey stick! I want a honey stick!

BERTHA BLACK BEAR: Children, children, mind your manners! We have a guest! Won't you sit down and share our birthday festivities?

MAGNUS FOURPENNY: (lowers shotgun, scratches his head) Wellllll . . . I reckon it can't be worse than what's waiting for me at home.

(AUNT BETTY BLACK BEAR and UNCLE BUCK BLACK BEAR lumber into den from stage left.)

BEAR CUBS: Hi, Aunt Betty and Uncle Buck!

AUNT BETTY BLACK BEAR: Howwwwww-dyyyyyy!

UNCLE BUCK BLACK BEAR: Hello, cubs! Happy birthday! *(points to MAGNUS)* Say, who's the biped?

BERTHA BLACK BEAR: Uncle Buck, this is our guest! Mister—

MAGNUS FOURPENNY: Magnus Fourpenny, ma'am. I was just passing through and thought I heard a party in progress.

UNCLE BUCK BLACK BEAR: Gatecrasher, eh? Haw-haw-haw! Well, here—take a load off your feet!

(UNCLE BUCK gives MAGNUS an enormous "bear hug," picking him up and setting him down again.)

MAGNUS FOURPENNY: Golly, I think that popped my dislocated rib joint back into place.

AUNT BETTY BLACK BEAR: He's like a cub; he doesn't know his own strength sometimes.

BUDDY BLACK BEAR: Hey, who wants to play a game?

BEAR CUB #1: I do! I do!

BEAR CUB #2: Pin the nose on the gopher!

BEAR CUB #3: Hide and seek! Hide and seek! *(swats MAGNUS in the arm)* Tag! You're it!

(BEAR CUBS scamper around stage as MAGNUS puts his hands over his eyes and begins counting.)

MAGNUS FOURPENNY: One, two, three, four, five, six, seven, eight—ready or not, here I come!

(CUBS dash offstage as Magnus opens eyes and gives chase. LIGHTS OUT BRIEFLY, THEN UP AGAIN. BEARS have exited left; MAGNUS stands center left; RUBY, the THREE FOURPENNY CHILDREN, AUNT MINNIE, UNCLE OWEN and OLD DOG SAM sit and stand around the table at right. CHILDREN sing to melody of Twinkle, Twinkle Little Star:)

CHILDREN: *(sing)*
Poppa, Poppa home he came
Empty-handed without game
Momma, momma got so red
Thought she'd up and bust his head

(Hands clasped in prayer, MAGNUS stands before RUBY who menacingly wields a frying pan.)

MAGNUS FOURPENNY: *(sings)*
There is no bear that I could shoot
Who shared with me his birthday loot

(Ruby turns away, disgusted.)

CHILDREN: *(sing)*
Poppa, he had so much fun
Says he'll throw away his gun
OLD DOG SAM: Arooo! Arooo! Arf-arf arooo!

(MAGNUS hands his shotgun to OLD DOG SAM.)

MAGNUS FOURPENNY: Go, Sam, go! Bury the gun! Bury the gun!

(OLD DOG SAM exits, lumbers off left.)

MAGNUS FOURPENNY: And, kids: bring out the shovels and the seed packets. We're going to plant a garden!
CHILDREN: Yayyyyy! A garden!

(THE FOURPENNY CHILDREN grab shovel and rake and hoe; MAGNUS directs them in gardening tasks as RUBY stands in place, waving the frying pan.)

RUBY FOURPENNY: Magnus Fourpenny, I sure hope you have better luck with vegetables than you do with bears.
UNCLE OWEN: And from that day on, Magnus Fourpenny never went hunting again.
AUNT MINNIE: He never had to. The garden Magnus planted grew the biggest and best-tastingest vegetables in all of Hardin County. Why, folks came from as far away as Louisiana and Arkansas to buy his produce. Magnus and his family became rich in no time at all.
UNCLE OWEN: Oh, he still liked to walk in the woods down by Gumstick Pond now and then. About once a year, he said. Just to play a game of hide and seek with some friends—who lived in a tree trunk.

(BEAR FAMILY enters from left and joins entire cast singing to melody of Twinkle, Twinkle Little Star *(final phrase with a coda), as AUNT MINNIE and UNCLE OWEN "conduct" the audience:)*

CAST: *(sing)*
　　Now it's time to say goodnight
　　To bears and children, sleeping tight
　　Sleep tight, star bright, say goodnight
　　(spoken) Goodnight!

(LIGHTS OUT.)

THE END

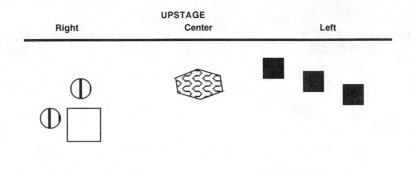

UPSTAGE

Right   Center   Left

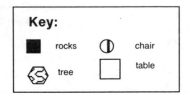

Stage Plan *Magnus Fourpenny and the Black Bear Birthday Bash*

Key:

■ rocks   ◐ chair

🌳 tree   ☐ table

THE LAZIEST GIRL IN THE WORLD

The Laziest Girl in the World is an old Irish folktale seen here in an American setting. As in many Irish legends, a person with an insurmountable task receives invaluable assistance from the *fairies*—small, mischievous supernatural beings usually invisible to human eyes but who, nonetheless, take an active interest in human affairs. Belief in fairies (or *brownies, pixies, sprites*, etc.) is common throughout the globe and is especially strong in Ireland, where many trees, rocks or old houses in the Irish countryside are said even today to be fairy "forts" or "circles"—inhabited by fairy spirits such as *leprechauns, banshees, clúracáns* and *pookas.*

TIME: 1890s—"The Mauve Decade"

PLACE: Boston, Massachusetts

CAST: Mrs. McDermott   First Old Woman
         Eileen O'Leary   Second Old Woman
         Eileen's Mother   Third Old Woman
         Mayor's Son   Butler
         Mayor   8 Wedding Guests
         Mayor's Wife   Fiddler

STAGE SET:chair; kitchen table; two stools; coat rack; clothes line; settee; spinning wheel (or sewing machine or weaving loom)

PROPS: teacup; umbrella; dustpan; cleaning rag; dishes; pots; pans; hanging clothes; bucket; broom; butler's handkerchief; large magnifying glass; basket; paper with shirt measurements; bridal veil; flower bouquet

COSTUMES: 1890s' dress for all characters reflecting occupation and social status; the Three Old Women wear different-colored shawls and long Irish peasant dresses (i.e. one blue, one green, one red)

(LIGHTS UP FULL; at stage right MRS. MCDERMOTT sits on a chair, drinking a cup of tea. She greets the audience)

MRS. MCDERMOTT: Saints above, I love a wedding! And I'm not the only one around here who does, you know. Didn't nearly the whole city of Boston turn out for Eileen O'Leary's wedding last month? What's that you say, love? You weren't there? Faith, come sit and have a cup of tea with Maisie McDermott, and I'll tell you all about it.

(EILEEN O'LEARY and EILEEN'S MOTHER enter from right, EILEEN'S MOTHER using a dustpan to gently prod EILEEN ahead to down left in front of kitchen table where EILEEN stops, fold her arms in front of her and assumes a very petulant expression.)

EILEEN'S MOTHER: Eileen O'Leary, you are the laziest girl in the whole world! I don't know what I am going to do with you! Look at this house; it's a mess, and you won't do a single thing to help clean it up!

EILEEN: I'm sorry, mother. But it's too lovely a day to do housework. We should both be out in the fields, picking flowers and dancing in the breeze. *(mimes actions of picking and dancing, then stops as her mother scowls)* But you won't have to worry about me for long—I'm going to get married.

EILEEN'S MOTHER: Eileen O'Leary, you must be daft! Why, there's no doubt you're a pretty lass…and well-spoken and bright…and possessed of a fine sense of Irish humor. But, daughter, you are simply the laziest girl in the world! You'll never find a man to marry you!

EILEEN: *(stamps her foot)* I will, so! And I'll find him today!

EILEEN'S MOTHER: *(puts dustpan and rag in EILEEN'S hands)* You won't find anyone till you finish cleaning this kitchen. Promise you'll have everything spick-and-span when I get home from work tonight?

EILEEN: *(sullenly)* I'll do my best.

EILEEN'S MOTHER: *(sighs)* Unfortunately, I believe you will. *(takes umbrella from coat rack and exits left)*

(EILEEN sets about tidying up the dishes and pots and pans stacked on the table.)

MRS. MCDERMOTT: Now, because Eileen was unaccustomed to housework, it meant that when she *did* start in to clean, she didn't rightly know how to go about it.

(One after another, EILEEN accidentally knocks stacks of pots, pans and dishes onto the floor.)

EILEEN: Oh no! Whoops! Ohmygosh!

(EILEEN grabs a broom to sweep, but the broom breaks in half; she backs up and kicks over a bucket; she stumbles around amid pots, pans and dishes, knocking over the stool and reeling into the clothesline, bringing it—and her—down onto the floor. EILEEN'S MOTHER enters from left and stands in shock, staring at the mess, as EILEEN struggles up.)

MRS. MCDERMOTT: By the time her mother came home, poor Eileen had upset every single item in the whole house.

EILEEN'S MOTHER: Eileen! You've turned this house upside down from one end to the other!

EILEEN: *(tearfully)* I did my best.

EILEEN'S MOTHER: *(shakes umbrella)* And may St. Patrick forgive me for what I'm about to do!

(She chases EILEEN around the stage, never catching her. After a few seconds of chase, a well-dressed young man (THE MAYOR'S SON) enters from stage right and watches the chase, unobserved. SOUND CUE: The Irish Washwoman played offstage on fiddle (or record) until MAYOR'S SON speaks.)

MRS. MCDERMOTT: And Mrs. O'Leary chased poor Eileen all through the house and all through the yard outside and had almost caught her—when at that very moment a young man happened to walk by.

MAYOR'S SON: I say there, madam: why are you chasing that young girl?

(EILEEN and EILEEN'S MOTHER freeze, then EILEEN'S MOTHER steps belligerently toward the young man.)

EILEEN'S MOTHER: And who is it who wants to know?

MAYOR'S SON: Only I, Harrison Trumble the Third, eldest son of the Mayor of Boston.

EILEEN'S MOTHER: *(laughs)* Oh, the son of the Mayor of Boston, he says! *(freezes, then hugs EILEEN in fright)*

EILEEN & EILEEN'S MOTHER: *(shout)* The son of the Mayor of Boston!

MRS. MCDERMOTT: Neither Eileen nor her mother could believe their eyes. For not only was this one of the richest man in all of Boston, he was one of the handsomest.

MAYOR'S SON: You don't have to shout, ladies. I simply asked, Why are you chasing that young girl? That very beautiful...very charming young girl. *(tips his hat to Eileen, who smiles and curtseys)*

MRS. MCDERMOTT: Of course, Mrs. O'Leary couldn't very well tell the Mayor's Son she was chasing Eileen because her daughter was the laziest girl in the world, could she? So, she replied with the first thing that came to her mind.

EILEEN'S MOTHER: *(chuckles)* Well, you see, sir: my daughter Eileen is *such* a hard worker, that if I didn't chase her around the yard every so often to make her stop working, she'd work herself to death!

MAYOR'S SON: Really?

(EILEEN and EILEEN'S MOTHER smile and shake their heads "yes"; MAYOR'S SON walks to EILEEN and takes her hand.)

MAYOR'S SON: I've been looking for a girl just like that. A hard-working girl—to be my wife. May I take your daughter to meet my parents?

(EILEEN and EILEEN'S MOTHER shrug their shoulders and grin; the MAYOR'S SON leads EILEEN by the hand to center stage, and they smile at each other; EILEEN'S MOTHER exits right; the MAYOR and MAYOR'S WIFE enter from left, accompanied by their BUTLER, who vigorously dusts the settee before they sit on it, then stands at the side of the MAYOR. MAYOR'S SON walks EILEEN to within a few feet of his parents and bows.)

MAYOR'S SON: Mother, Father...I have met the girl I want to marry. Meet Eileen O'Leary from South Boston.

(The BUTLER takes EILEEN'S hand and walks her to the MAYOR who shakes her hand, then to the MAYOR'S WIFE who shakes her hand, then back beside the MAYOR'S SON.)

MAYOR: *(stands)* As Mayor of Boston, I hereby declare Eileen O'Leary as beautiful as the Rose of Tralee and as sweet as Tullamore Dew. If she's as hard-working as you say she is, son, why she'll make you a perfect wife.

MAYOR'S WIFE: *(stands with BUTLER'S help)* Not so fast, husband. *(BUTLER takes off her gloves)* What proof do we have that this is a hard-working girl? *(BUTLER hands her a large magnifying glass, through which she stares at EILEEN)* The last thing we want in this family is someone who can't fend for themselves. *(BUTLER takes the glass and helps her sit down)* Perhaps we should give your future bride a test of her working skills?

MAYOR'S SON: Very well, mother. I accept.

EILEEN: Now, wait a minute, Harrison—

MAYOR'S SON: And so does Eileen.

(With BUTLER'S assistance, MAYOR'S WIFE rises and takes EILEEN by the hand; the three of them cross to mid right to a spinning wheel (or sewing machine) and basket; MAYOR and MAYOR'S SON remain at center stage.)

MAYOR'S WIFE: To marry my son, Miss O'Leary, you must pass three tests. First, you must sit at this spinning wheel and spin all the flax in this basket into fine linen.

EILEEN: *(looks in basket)* In that basket? Why, there must be a hundred pounds of flax in that basket!

MAYOR'S WIFE: *(turns away)* By tomorrow morning, no later. Butler will stand guard outside the door to make sure you're not disturbed during the night.

(MAYOR'S WIFE exits and returns to sit on settee; BUTLER walks forward a few steps as if passing through a door, locks the "door," turns and stands at parade rest in front of door; EILEEN sits on stool.)

MRS. MCDERMOTT: Now poor Eileen was really in a fix. She'd never spun flax before, because—truth be told—she'd been too lazy to learn how to work a spinning wheel.

EILEEN: I knew I should have taken home economics in junior high! Oh, what am I going to do? I'll never spin all this flax by morning! *(sobs)*

(FIRST OLD WOMAN enters from up right, creeping stealthily up to EILEEN, who does not immediately see her.)

MRS. MCDERMOTT: And at that moment, a wee old woman crept in through the window. She looked at Eileen…and the basket of flax …and the spinning wheel…and then back at Eileen again before she spoke.

FIRST OLD WOMAN: Eileen O'Leary!

EILEEN: *(jumps up, startled)* Who …who are you?

FIRST OLD WOMAN: Randelum-fandelum, high-diddle-dandelum; randelum-fandelum, high-diddle-dee!

EILEEN: My goodness, that's a very unusual name. But very lovely. You wouldn't happen to know anything about spinning flax, would you?

(The OLD WOMAN pushes EILEEN away from the spinning wheel, dips into the basket and begins spinning the flax as EILEEN goes to sleep.)

FIRST OLD WOMAN: Randelum-fandelum, high-diddle-dandelum; randelum-fandelum, high-diddle-dee! Randelum-fandelum, high-diddle-dandelum; randelum-fandelum, high-diddle-dee! Randelum-fandelum, high-diddle-dandelum; randelum-fandelum, high-diddle-dee!

(OLD WOMAN stops spinning and stealthily creeps out of "window" (exits up right); EILEEN awakes.)

MRS. MCDERMOTT: And in the morning, Eileen awoke to find that every single bit of flax in the basket had been spun into beautiful linen.

EILEEN: Mrs. Mayor! Oh, Mrs. Mayor!

BUTLER: Mrs. Mayor! Mrs. Mayor to the spinning room!

(MAYOR'S WIFE crosses to spinning room and looks into basket.)

EILEEN: Look! All the flax has been spun! Every bit!

(MAYOR and MAYOR'S SON shake hands, slap shoulders congratulating each other.)

MAYOR'S WIFE: This is truly remarkable! Very nearly incredible! But we'll see how you do with Test Number Two. You must sit at this weaving loom and weave all the linen in this basket into fine cloth.

EILEEN: *(looks in basket)* By tomorrow morning, I suppose?

MAYOR'S WIFE: *(turns away)* Butler will stand guard outside the door to make sure you're not disturbed during the night.

(MAYOR'S WIFE exits and returns to sit on settee; BUTLER walks forward a few steps as if passing through a door, locks the "door," turns and stands at parade rest in front of door; EILEEN sits on stool.)

EILEEN: Now I'm surely undone! I don't know *how* to weave! *(sobs)*

(SECOND OLD WOMAN enters from up right, creeping stealthily up to EILEEN, who does not immediately see her.)

MRS. MCDERMOTT: And at that moment, *another* wee old woman crept in through the window. She looked at Eileen…and the basket of linen…and the weaving loom…and then back at Eileen again before she spoke.

SECOND OLD WOMAN: Eileen O'Leary!

EILEEN: *(jumps up, startled)* Who…who are you?

SECOND OLD WOMAN: With my too-roo-roo, rubba-diddle-doo; too-rum-roo ry-er-o!

EILEEN: Well, I'd never have guessed on my own. As long as you're here, could I ask you a question about linen weaving?

(The OLD WOMAN pushes EILEEN away from the weaving loom, dips into the basket and begins weaving the linen as EILEEN goes to sleep.)

SECOND OLD WOMAN:
With my too-roo-roo, rubba-diddle-doo; too-rum-roo ry-er-o!
With my too-roo-roo, rubba-diddle-doo; too-rum-roo ry-er-o!
With my too-roo-roo, rubba-diddle-doo; too-rum-roo ry-er-o!

(OLD WOMAN stops weaving and stealthily creeps out of window (exits up right); EILEEN awakes.)

The Laziest Girl in the World 89

MRS. MCDERMOTT: And in the morning, Eileen awoke to find that the second wee old woman had woven every single strand of linen into beautiful cloth.

EILEEN: Mrs. Mayor! Oh, Mrs. Mayor!

BUTLER: Mrs. Mayor! Mrs. Mayor to the weaving room!

(MAYOR'S WIFE crosses to weaving room and looks into basket.)

EILEEN: Look! All the linen has been woven! Every strand!

(MAYOR and MAYOR'S SON shake hands, slap shoulders congratulating each other.)

MAYOR'S WIFE: It would appear that you are indeed a hard-working girl. Here is your final test. You must sit at this sewing machine and sew all the cloth in this basket into a shirt for my son. *(thrusts a paper into EILEEN'S hands)* These are his measurements.

EILEEN: *(looks at paper)* By tomorrow morning, I suppose?

MAYOR'S WIFE: *(turns away)* Eight a.m. sharp. Butler!

(MAYOR'S WIFE exits and returns to sit on settee; BUTLER walks to guard position; EILEEN sits on stool and begins sobbing.)

MRS. MCDERMOTT: Naturally, being the laziest girl in the world, Eileen had never bothered to learn a thing about sewing. And so she cried and cried and cried until she fell fast asleep.

(THIRD OLD WOMAN enters from up right, creeping stealthily up to EILEEN, who is asleep.)

MRS. MCDERMOTT: And it was then that a third wee old woman crept in through the window. And she went straight away to the sewing machine without bothering to wake up Eileen or tell anyone her name at all.

(The OLD WOMAN stands at sewing machine and begins sewing.)

THIRD OLD WOMAN:
Whack for the toora loora laddie, whack for the toora loora-eh
Whack for the toora loora laddie, whack for the toora loora-eh
Whack for the toora loora laddie, whack for the toora loora-eh

(OLD WOMAN stops sewing and stealthily creeps out of window (exits up right); EILEEN awakes.)

MRS. MCDERMOTT: And when Eileen awoke at daybreak, there was the linen sewn into a beautiful handmade shirt.

EILEEN: *(runs past BUTLER to center stage brandishing shirt)* Mrs. Mayor! Oh, Mrs. Mayor!

MAYOR'S WIFE: *(turns away)* Don't tell me!

MAYOR: Why, it's got pearl buttons and French cuffs!

EILEEN: *(gives shirt to MAYOR'S SON)* Here you are, my love.

MAYOR'S SON: *(takes shirt)* You are a hard-working girl! And now you'll be my wife! Come on, everyone! Let the wedding begin!

(EIGHT WEDDING GUESTS enter from left; EILEEN'S MOTHER and a FIDDLER enter from right. SOUND CUE: Haste to the Wedding played by FIDDLER. BUTLER places a bridal veil on EILEEN; a WEDDING GUEST hands her a flower bouquet; everyone dances an Irish jig.)

MRS. MCDERMOTT: And that was how the laziest girl in the world got married to a rich and handsome man. Those wee old women were fairies, don't you see? Someone in Eileen's family long ago must have done a great service to them, and now they were returning the favor to her. But if you ask me, it only goes to show that if luck can get you into trouble, it can get you out just as quick.

(LIGHTS OUT.)

THE END

Haste to the Wedding

The Irish Washwoman

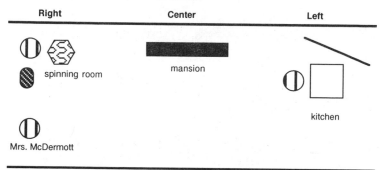

UPSTAGE

| Right | Center | Left |

spinning room

mansion

kitchen

Mrs. McDermott

Stage Plan *The Laziest Girl in the World*

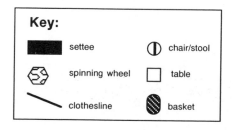

Key:

	settee		chair/stool
	spinning wheel		table
	clothesline		basket

TILLIE EDELPICKEL'S SACK OF LIES

Tillie Edelpickel's Sack of Lies comes from the folklore tradition of the Pennsylvania Dutch, emigrants from Germany, Switzerland and Moravia who first settled in southeastern Pennsylvania in the early 1700s. Despite their name, the Pennsylvania Dutch do not come from Holland. In the German tongue, "Deutsch" is the word for "German"; when English-speaking Americans first heard these German-speaking settlers referring to their language as "Deutsch," they took to calling them "Dutch," and the term has stuck to this day. Much German culture and folklore is still in evidence throughout Pennsylvania Dutch country, where many folk-tales feature the descendants of a mischievous figure named Till Eulen-spiegel, a character in numerous medieval German stories who uses jests and tricks to outwit his foes. In *Tillie Edelpickel's Sack of Lies*, the prankster has become a girl, Tillie, who is, nevertheless, as resolutely clever as her male predecessors in standing up to danger and tyranny.

TIME: November, 1776

PLACE: Lancaster County, Pennsylvania

CAST: Tillie Edelpickel   Colonel Jimsby
         Peter Edelpickel   Lady Jimsby
         Goat   Young Master Jimsby
         Goat Tender   Young Mistress Jimsby
         Hexfrau   Three British Soldiers
         Hangman   Six American Soldiers
         General George Washington

PROPS: battle plans; tinwhistle; knapsack; four money purses; pistol; ring; locket; sack; rifles and swords for soldiers; hangman's noose

COSTUMES: late 18th-century Colonial country dress for Tillie, Peter, Hexfrau, Goat Tender; standard Revolutionary War military uniforms for British and American soldiers; fancy dress for Lady Jimsby, Young Master Jimsby and Young Mistress Jimsby; goat mask/costume for Goat

(LIGHTS UP FULL; PETER EDELPICKEL enters from stage right, creeping and scurrying stealthily around the stage from up right to up left and to down center. BRITISH SOLDIER #1 enters behind him from stage left and points his rifle at him.)

BRITISH SOLDIER #1: Halt! Who goes there?

(PETER freezes but does not turn.)

PETER: A poor wayfaring pilgrim seeking shelter from the evening's bitter cold.

BRITISH SOLDIER #1: State the password!

(PETER turns to face soldier and does not see BRITISH SOLDIER #2 entering behind him from stage right.)

PETER: Password? Uh, let's see…password…how about "King George the Third is an Old Rotten Crab Apple"? Yaaah!!!

(PETER turns to flee right but is confronted by BRITISH SOLDIER #2.)

BRITISH SOLDIER #2: Stop right where you are, rebel! Colonel Jimsby! Come quick! We have a Yankee spy!

(COLONEL JIMSBY and BRITISH SOLDIER #3 enter from stage left followed by LADY JIMSBY, YOUNG MASTER JIMSBY and YOUNG MISTRESS JIMSBY; BRITISH SOLDIER #1 searches PETER'S jacket as TILLIE EDELPICKEL, carrying a knapsack, enters unseen from stage right and quietly observes.)

PETER: I'm no spy! And I'm no Connecticut Yankee, either. My name is Peter Edelpickel, and I'm pure Pennsylvania Dutch from the heart of Lancaster County. Where you British are trespassing! Say, give that back!

(BRITISH SOLDIER #1 pulls a crumpled piece of paper from PETER'S jacket and hands it to COLONEL JIMSBY, who briefly inspects it.)

COLONEL JIMSBY: Not a spy, eh? Please explain, my young Colonial firebrand, what these battle plans for His Majesty's Infantry are doing in your possession?

PETER: I...I...I found them in my Uncle Jacob's haystack.

COLONEL JIMSBY: Then your uncle is a traitor as well. And your sentence, as well as his when we find him, shall be that of all traitors to his majesty the King of England—death by hanging.

TILLIE: No! *(runs forward to face COLONEL and is stopped at bayonet-point by BRITISH SOLDIER #3)*

COLONEL JIMSBY: And who is this impertinent young creature?

TILLIE: I am Tillie Edelpickel, the sister of this young boy you have condemned to die. Please, spare his life!

(COLONEL JIMSBY, his FAMILY and the BRITISH SOLDIERS laugh.)

COLONEL JIMSBY: Spare his life? Surely you jest! Ever since those madmen in Philadelphia declared their independence last July, you colonials have had the wildest flights of fancy. Corporal, fetch the hangman!

YOUNG MASTER JIMSBY: *(steps forward)* Father, wait. I admire the spirit of this country lass. Can we not make a more sporting proposition of this affair?

YOUNG MISTRESS JIMSBY: Yes, father, do! Why don't we give her a task to perform?

COLONEL JIMSBY: A task? What do you say, Lady Jimsby?

LADY JIMSBY: Hmmm...she appears to be a clever girl, though frightfully dressed. A milkmaid or stockherd by profession, no doubt. Why not let her be useful? Give her a goat to take to the mountains. She must set the goat free and let it graze. In thirty days, she must bring it back, fattened and ready for our Christmas dinner.

PETER: Grazing a goat in the middle of winter? Why, that's not possible!

TILLIE: Anything is possible when my brother's life is at stake.

COLONEL JIMSBY: Very well, then. You have your task. We shall stay the execution for thirty days. Corporal, secure the prisoner.

(GOAT TENDER enters from right trailing GOAT, and brings GOAT to TILLIE; BRITISH SOLDIERS march PETER offstage left, followed by COLONEL JIMSBY and FAMILY.)

GOAT TENDER: There you go, fraulein. His name is Benedict.

TILLIE: Benedict? That's a peculiar name for a goat.

GOAT TENDER: Named after Benedict Arnold. He's a peculiar general. *(exits right)*

(Hands on her hips, TILLIE stares at the GOAT for several seconds; GOAT stares back.)

TILLIE: I am doomed! As soon as I let you loose in the mountains, you will run away. And my brother will be hung! *(cries)*

GOAT: Baa-aaa-aaa!

(An old HEXFRAU enters from right and walks slowly across the stage, head bowed and back bent, face hidden in a black shawl; she stops in front of the weeping TILLIE.)

HEXFRAU: Fraulein, why do you cry?

TILLIE: Pardon me, Hexfrau, but I must graze this goat for thirty days, then bring him back to the British Colonel—or my brother will be hung. How can I do this in the middle of winter when grass is so scarce?

HEXFRAU: You cannot. *(takes a tinwhistle from her shawl)* Not without this magic whistle and the magic words that go with it. *(hands tinwhistle to TILLIE)* Whenever you want the goat to come back to you, blow on this whistle and say these words:

> In mountain high and valley low
> Fourteen angels with me go
> Two at the head, two at the foot
> Two at the left, two at the right
> Two to cover me, two to wake me
> Two to guide me into the heavenly paradise, amen

TILLIE: Oh, Hexfrau, I am in your debt forever. How can I ever repay you?

HEXFRAU: By making sure the British are defeated and our United States of America become free for all people of the world! *(shuffles offstage left)*

TILLIE: Well there, Mr. Benedict. You heard the hexfrau. Let's go to the mountain and graze.

(TILLIE and the GOAT amble around stage for several seconds, GOAT "baa-aaa-aaa" ing; YOUNG MASTER JIMSBY enters from left.)

YOUNG MASTER JIMSBY: I say there, young lady. You've been out here in the mountains for seven days. How is your goat?

TILLIE: He is doing well, I think.

YOUNG MASTER JIMSBY: Excellent. I would like to buy him. I will offer you thirty silver shillings. That's ten times what that old bag of bones is worth.

TILLIE: Young Master Jimsby, how could you ever suggest such a thing? If I sell you this goat, my brother will be hung!

YOUNG MASTER JIMSBY: Fifty shillings, then!

TILLIE: And that shiny new pistol you're carrying?

YOUNG MASTER JIMSBY: Sold!

(He takes pistol from belt and gives it to her; takes a money purse and gives it to her.)

YOUNG MASTER JIMSBY: Come on, you old horn-head! *(takes GOAT offstage right)*

TILLIE:

In mountain high and valley low
Fourteen angels with me go
Two at the head, two at the foot
Two at the left, two at the right
Two to cover me, two to wake me
Two to guide me into the heavenly paradise, amen

(She blows the tinwhistle; GOAT comes bounding back; YOUNG MISTRESS JIMSBY enters from left.)

YOUNG MISTRESS JIMSBY: Why, hello, Tillie. Imagine meeting you here. How long now since you've been grazing your goat?

TILLIE: Fourteen days, I think.

YOUNG MISTRESS JIMSBY: That is so long to be out in the mountains. You're missing all the wonderful parties in town. If you sell him to me, I will pay you twenty gold guineas, and you can go home.

TILLIE: Young Mistress Jimsby, how could you ever suggest such a thing? If I sell you this goat, my brother will be hung!

YOUNG MISTRESS JIMSBY: Sixty guineas, then! And this beautiful gold locket, if you like.

TILLIE: Hand it over!

(YOUNG MISTRESS JIMSBY gives money purse and locket to TILLIE, who drops them both in her knapsack.)

YOUNG MISTRESS JIMSBY: Come on, Mr. Fuzzy Knickers! *(takes GOAT offstage right)*

TILLIE:
> In mountain high and valley low
> Fourteen angels with me go
> Two at the head, two at the foot
> Two at the left, two at the right
> Two to cover me, two to wake me
> Two to guide me into the heavenly paradise, amen

(She blows the tinwhistle; GOAT comes bounding back; LADY JIMSBY enters from left.)

LADY JIMSBY: Oh, it's you, the goat girl. Why, you've been out in the wilderness now for twenty-one days.

TILLIE: I am so very tired, I think.

LADY JIMSBY: You look absolutely exhausted. Sell the goat to me, and I will give you this bag of precious rubies.

TILLIE: I could never do such a thing…unless you give me that wedding ring on your finger.

LADY JIMSBY: You drive a hard bargain. Very well. But, please don't tell my husband, the Colonel.

TILLIE: I wouldn't dream of it, my lady.

(LADY JIMSBY gives jewel purse and ring to TILLIE, who drops them both in her knapsack.)

LADY JIMSBY: Come along, Sir Goat! Your Christmas dinner awaits. *(takes GOAT offstage right)*

TILLIE:
> In mountain high and valley low
> Fourteen angels with me go
> Two at the head, two at the foot
> Two at the left, two at the right
> Two to cover me, two to wake me
> Two to guide me into the heavenly paradise, amen

(She blows the tinwhistle; GOAT comes bounding back; COLONEL JIMSBY enters from left.)

COLONEL JIMSBY: Miss Edelpickel, you've been a formidable foe. You have nearly completed your time.

TILLIE: Twenty-eight days, I think.

COLONEL JIMSBY: If you come back with that fattened goat, I will look a complete fool in front of my troops. Please let me buy it from you for one hundred pounds sterling.

TILLIE: Oh, Colonel Jimsby, I could never do that. Unless we made an exchange.

COLONEL JIMSBY: Exchange?

TILLIE: Something of equal value to my brother's life—the battle plans for His Majesty's Infantry.

COLONEL JIMSBY: Impossible!

TILLIE: No plans, no goat.

COLONEL JIMSBY: You may have the better of me now, but I shall have the better of you yet.

(COLONEL JIMSBY gives money purse and batlle plan paper to TILLIE, who drops them both in her knapsack.)

COLONEL JIMSBY: Ten-shun! Right face! Forward march! *(takes GOAT offstage right)*

TILLIE:
In mountain high and valley low
Fourteen angels with me go
Two at the head, two at the foot
Two at the left, two at the right
Two to cover me, two to wake me
Two to guide me into the heavenly paradise, amen

(She blows the tinwhistle; GOAT comes bounding back; COLONEL JIMSBY enters from left with THREE BRITISH SOLDIERS, LADY JIMSBY, YOUNG MASTER JIMSBY, YOUNG MISTRESS JIMSBY and THE HANGMAN leading PETER and swinging a noose; all convene at center stage.)

TILLIE: Good day, all! My thirty days a-grazing have passed. I give to you this fattened goat. Now give to me my brother.

COLONEL JIMSBY: You say you grazed that goat for thirty days?

TILLIE: I did, it's true.

COLONEL JIMSBY: You lie. You switched it for another that looks alike. What have you in that sack?

TILLIE: Lies, all lies.

COLONEL JIMSBY: Then fill it up!

(TILLIE puts her knapsack on the ground; every time someone says "Fill it up!", she mimes plucking an object from the air and stuffing it into the sack.)

TILLIE: First lie: Colonel says I switched the goats.

THREE BRITISH SOLDIERS: Fill it up!

TILLIE: On the seventh day, a man came to me on the mountain and asked to buy my goat! It was Young Master Jimsby.

YOUNG MASTER JIMSBY: You lie!

THREE BRITISH SOLDIERS: Fill it up!

COLONEL JIMSBY: How do you know it was my son?

TILLIE: Because he gave me this new pistol. (*shows pistol*)

YOUNG MASTER JIMSBY: You lie!

THREE BRITISH SOLDIERS: Fill it up!

TILLIE: On the fourteenth day, Young Mistress Jimsby asked to buy my goat!

YOUNG MISTRESS JIMSBY: You lie!

THREE BRITISH SOLDIERS: Fill it up!

YOUNG MISTRESS JIMSBY: How do you know it was I?

TILLIE: Because you gave me this gold locket.

YOUNG MISTRESS JIMSBY: You lie!

THREE BRITISH SOLDIERS: Fill it up!

TILLIE: On the twenty-first day, Lady Jimsby asked to buy my goat!

LADY JIMSBY: You lie!

THREE BRITISH SOLDIERS: Fill it up!

LADY JIMSBY: How dare you say 'twas me?

TILLIE: Because you gave me this wedding ring.

LADY JIMSBY: You lie!

THREE BRITISH SOLDIERS: Fill it up!

TILLIE: On the twenty-eighth day, Colonel Jimsby asked to buy my goat!

COLONEL JIMSBY: You lie!

THREE BRITISH SOLDIERS: Fill it up!

COLONEL JIMSBY: Can't you see she's mad?

TILLIE: And you gave me these battle plans for His Majesty's Infantry.

COLONEL JIMSBY: You lie!

THREE BRITISH SOLDIERS: Fill it up!

TILLIE: The British are going to invade Valley Forge!

COLONEL JIMSBY: You lie!

THREE BRITISH SOLDIERS: Fill it up!

(GENERAL GEORGE WASHINGTON and SIX AMERICAN SOL-DIERS enter from right, unobserved.)

TILLIE: But General George Washington will save the day!

COLONEL JIMSBY: You lie!

SIX AMERICAN SOLDIERS: Fill it up!

(BRITISH SOLDIERS, COLONEL and his FAMILY are startled and start to run offstage left but are captured by AMERICAN SOLDIERS.)

GEORGE WASHINGTON: You can't escape, Colonel. The Continental Army you so despise has you surrounded. Now, free this bold young man immediately.

SIX AMERICAN SOLDIERS: Hurrah for General Washington and the United States of America!

(PETER is released by HANGMAN and shakes WASHINGTON'S hand, then embraces TILLIE.)

COLONEL JIMSBY: General Washington! What an unpleasant surprise. I thought you were dug in for the winter at Valley Forge.

GEORGE WASHINGTON: We were, until Fraulein Edelpickel sent us word of your plans to attack. This brave young lass has saved the nation in its darkest hour.

SIX AMERICAN SOLDIERS: Hurrah for Tillie Edelpickel and the United States of America!

COLONEL JIMSBY: Well done, General. I suppose you'll be taking that animal as well. That blasted billy-goat should make tasty cutlets for at least a company or two.

GEORGE WASHINGTON: Release that animal! No, Colonel, King George may eat billy-goat for his Christmas dinner, but here in America, we'll stick to turkey.

SIX AMERICAN SOLDIERS: Hurrah for turkey dinner and the United States of America!

(LIGHTS OUT.)

THE END

THE GLASS MOUNTAIN

The Glass Mountain is based upon a Finnish-American tale from the Upper Peninsula of Michigan, where many immigrants from Finland settled during the late 19th century to work in the region's iron mines and lumber camps. *The Glass Mountain* belongs to a tale type known as *märchen*, a type that includes stories like *Snow White, Faithful John, The Frog Prince* and *Cinderella*, of which this is a variant. The motif of the hero having to climb something high and forbidding is found around the world: in India the mountain is a high palisade, among Slavic nations a high tower. The *noita* who helps Tukimo is an important figure in ancient Finnish peasant culture. A noita is a healer who cures the sick and charms and curses evildoers to defend his people against enemies. Sometimes, as in this tale, the noita offers a bit of friendly assistance to help give an underdog the upper hand.

TIME: About a hundred years ago

PLACE: A small mining village in Northern Michigan

CAST:

Narrator	3 Suitors
Company Boss	Maki, the Noita
Boss' Wife	Heikki the Horse
Boss' Daughter	Architect
Tukimo (Cinders)	3 Architect Assistants
Kalami (Cinders' brother)	2 Mountain Guards
Kusta (Cinders' brother)	4 Daughter's Girlfriends
Newsboy	

STAGE SET: a "glass mountain" (a pyramid-shaped wooden structure 4-feet high, painted white with a flat top that has enough space for a person to sit on it; stair steps can be set into it so it can be easily ascended; should have wheels or be on a cart); a stool

PROPS: whittling knife; architect plans; scarves; "Help" sign; dice; golden apple; mop; newspaper; silver-painted sneakers; hand mirror

COSTUMES: Tukimo first appears in ragged work overalls; when he visits the glass mountain he is dressed in a flowing cape, fancy jacket, white gloves, etc.; the Boss and Boss' Wife are dressed in evening formal clothes, top hat for Boss and large flowered hat for Boss' Wife; all others wear late 19th-century clothes suitable to their class and occupation

(LIGHTS UP STAGE RIGHT on a stool where a NARRATOR sits, whittling a piece of wood. He looks at the audience.)

NARRATOR: Once upon a time up in the deep North Woods of Michigan, there was a man who owned a big iron mine. He owned a couple railroads, too, and even a lumber camp across Lake Superior in Canada. Yessir, he was the richest man in the whole county. Why, he and his wife used to give some of the biggest parties you ever saw!

(LIGHTS UP STAGE LEFT as the BOSS and his WIFE stroll out arm-in-arm from left, bowing and greeting imaginary partygoers.)

NARRATOR: But just because these two had a lot of money, you shouldn't think they didn't have problems like ordinary folk. They had a very big problem—they had a lovely, lovely daughter.

(LIGHTS UP CENTER on DAUGHTER, seated on a stool at the edge of the stage, primping in a hand mirror.)

NARRATOR: In addition to being very, very lovely, she was also very, very talented.

(DAUGHTER plays a few riffs on a musical instrument—clarinet, guitar, trumpet, sax, kazoo—anything (doesn't matter if it's played well or poorly); she stops when BOSS and BOSS' WIFE approach her and tap her on shoulder.)

NARRATOR: When she was of age, the boss and his wife decided it was time for their lovely daughter to get married. *(lowers voice)* I think they really wanted her out of the house.

DAUGHTER: *(whirls around and addresses NARRATOR)* I heard that!

BOSS: Of course, we're only thinking of your happiness, daughter dear.

BOSS' WIFE: Yes, darling, we want you to marry a gentleman. A man who is your equal in grace, breeding and intelligence.

BOSS: Naturally, a lot of yahoos—er, suitors—are going to try for your hand.

BOSS' WIFE: And our money.

BOSS: So, we've come up with a test to make sure the man who marries you is truly worthy.

DAUGHTER: *(jumps up, excited)* You're going to have him recite the complete plays of Shakespeare and play the *Star-Spangled Banner* on twelve different instruments? Then, to prove his sensitive and romantic nature, he's going to write me one hundred sonnets of love poetry and paint a gorgeous watercolor of the evening sun sinking over the horizon?

BOSS' WIFE: No, darling. We're going to build a tall mountain made of glass and sit you at the top. Whatever man can climb it will be the man you marry.

DAUGHTER: Are you people out of your minds? What kind of a test is that? I don't even *like* mountains! Why would I want to marry somebody that climbs them? Moth-errrrrr!

(BOSS' WIFE shrugs and walks upstage left, followed by DAUGHTER remonstrating with her; BOSS whistles in ARCHITECT, who rushes in from stage left with an armful of plans; ARCHITECT motions in 3 ASSISTANTS, who from stage left wheel in the glass mountain and position it at center stage under supervision of BOSS and ARCHITECT.)

NARRATOR: So the boss commissioned the finest architect in the land to build a big mountain made of glass—kind of like a skyscraper, only in the middle of the woods. Then, he built a small mansion on top of the mountain. And this is where the daughter went to live.

(ARCHITECT and ASSISTANTS exit left, as BOSS and BOSS' WIFE help/push DAUGHTER up the mountain; at the top, DAUGHTER sits, frowning and holding her head in her hands.)

BOSS: Believe me, dear, you'll be very happy here. We've brought your friends to keep you company.

(FOUR DAUGHTER'S GIRLFRIENDS enter from stage right, scurry across stage and sit on floor around the mountain, giggling and twirling scarves.)

DAUGHTER: *(to audience)* These twits are *not* my friends!

BOSS' WIFE: And, to protect you out here in the woods, we've hired security guards.

(TWO GUARDS [large, uniformed] enter from stage left, march across stage and take up position on either side of the mountain, facing audience; DAUGHTER'S GIRLFRIENDS ooh and aah at them, as BOSS and BOSS' WIFE step aside to the left. As they speak, DAUGHTER holds up a sign that says: "HELP!")

BOSS: Excellent! Now I'll send word out to all the swells and dandies in the country: whomever can climb up this rugged glass mountain—and get down again safely—can marry my daughter!

BOSS' WIFE: That's a very clever idea, darling. But what if one of these enterprising young men claims to have climbed the mountain but never did? How will we know if he's telling the truth?

BOSS: Oh. That is a stumper. Hmmm…

BOSS' WIFE: May I make a suggestion?

BOSS: Yes, of course, dear.

BOSS' WIFE: We give our daughter a golden apple. And she gives the apple to the man who succeeds in climbing the glass mountain.

BOSS: And when he comes back down with the golden apple—

BOSS' WIFE: We know it's truly him.

BOSS: Excellent! I'll send off to Tiffany's for a golden apple at once!

(BOSS and BOSS' WIFE go to curtain at stage right and watch as SUITOR #1 strolls in from stage left (DAUGHTER'S GIRLFRIENDS and GUARDS stand behind mountain); he gauges mountain, tries to climb but fails, sliding and falling, finally stumbling offstage right behind NARRATOR as SUITOR #2 strolls in from left, repeating his actions and followed by SUITOR #3.)

NARRATOR: Well, the high-society swells and dandies came from all over to see if they could marry the boss' daughter. But try as they might, not a single one of them could climb up the glass mountain. The boss and wife were getting worried. And the poor daughter was getting *really* bored.

(DAUGHTER yawns, puts her head on her knees; BOSS and BOSS' WIFE exit right. LIGHTS OUT CENTER STAGE; SPOTLIGHT UP STAGE LEFT on three boys standing at corner of stage. Two face the audience, the third faces away.)

NARRATOR: But a hundred miles away or so, almost to Wisconsin, lived a family of three brothers. The oldest was Kusta—

(KUSTA steps forward, bows, flexes arms, pounds chest, shows off his fine clothes.)

KUSTA: My name is Kusta, I'm cool as can be; if you wanna see some action, stick around with me!

NARRATOR: The second oldest was Kalami—

(KALAMI steps forward, pushing KUSTA aside, and bows, flexes arms, pounds chest, shows off his fine clothes.)

KALAMI: My name is Kalami, I'm the family stud; impressing the women, it's in my blood!

NARRATOR: And the youngest was Tukimo…

(Dressed in raggedy overalls and holding a mop, TUKIMO steps shyly forward; he smiles and starts to speak but is roughly shoved aside by his brothers who direct him to mop the stage.)

NARRATOR: …who was a very gentle boy, unlike his older brothers. Tukimo was also a hard worker, mainly because his brothers forced him to do all the housekeeping chores while they played silly games and frittered away their time.

(KUSTA and KALAMI primp, roll dice, laze on floor while TUKIMO mops, then yawns and lays down.)

NARRATOR: Tukimo was such a hard worker, he got very tired at night. So when it was bedtime, he just fell asleep on the hearth in front of the fireplace…and woke up all grimy and covered with ashes.

(KUSTA goes to TUKIMO and nudges him awake with his foot.)

KUSTA: *(snickering)* Hey, look—it's old Cinders!

KALAMI: *(guffaws)* Hey, bro', maybe you should try some ash-remover on your face.

(They laugh at TUKIMO and mock him, dancing around him and pointing.)

KUSTA & KALAMI:
> Cinders, Cinders, ashes in your hair
> Ashes in your ears, even in your underwear
> Ashes on your head, ashes on your toes
> Ashes in the air every time you blow your nose

(TUKIMO ignores them and takes a newspaper from his back pocket; he reads for a few seconds, then becomes excited and stands.)

TUKIMO: Hey, guys! Look at this! The biggest mine boss in the county is looking for a fella to marry his daughter. And all you have to do is climb up a glass mountain and climb back down again.

(KUSTA grabs newspaper from TUKIMO.)

KUSTA: Lemme see that!

(KALAMI grabs the paper from KUSTA.)

KALAMI: Hey! You can't read!

(KUSTA grabs paper back.)

KUSTA: Neither can you!

KALAMI: *(scratches his head)* Yeh, you're right. Hey, I'm gonna go marry that rich girl. My name is Kusta, I'm cool as can be; I'll climb that mountain in 1-2-3!

KALAMI: As if! My name is Kalami, I'm the family stud; I'll marry that girl, or my name is mud!

(LIGHTS UP CENTER STAGE. KUSTA and KALAMI cross to mountain while TUKIMO mops; KUSTA and KALAMI try to climb mountain as DAUGHTER'S GIRLFRIENDS cheer them on.)

GIRLFRIENDS: Come on, guys! Come on, you big manly men! Up! Up! Up!

(They align as a cheerleader squad.)

GIRLFRIENDS:
> Climb the mountain made of glass
> Then slide down upon your
> A-s-p-h-a-l-t

She's the girl you've sworn to free!
Up you went, down you came
Now go tumbling home again!
Goooooooo, brothers!

(KUSTA and KALAMI fail miserably, spraining their backs and ankles, and limp back to stage left; DAUGHTER'S GIRLFRIENDS flop down and moan.)

DAUGHTER: It's going to be a verrrrrr-y long winter...

(TUKIMO stops mopping and greets his brothers.)

TUKIMO: Hey, guys—how did the mountain climbing go?
KUSTA: Ahhh, shut up, squirt!
KALAMI: Take your mop and fly to the moon, cinder-man!

(KUSTA and KALAMI shuffle offstage left; TUKIMO lies down and sleeps. SPOTLIGHT STAGE RIGHT as the old noita MAKI creeps in from stage right, crosses to TUKIMO and bends over him, waving his hands about and making figures in the air. TUKIMO stirs awake.)

TUKIMO: Who are you?
MAKI: My name is Maki. I'm your noita.
TUKIMO: My what?
MAKI: Noita. N-o-i-t-a. I'm a mystical healer who cures the sick and charms and curses evildoers.
TUKIMO: That's cool.
MAKI: But I'm not real. I'm a bit of folklore from the old country. A mere figment of your imagination, a dream. In fact, you're not even awake right now.
TUKIMO: Oh...well, I better get back to sleep.
MAKI: But I can still tell you how to get up that glass mountain and marry the Boss' Beautiful Daughter.
TUKIMO: Really?
MAKI: Sure. First, let me introduce you to another figment of your nocturnal imagination—my horse, Heikki.

(HEIKKI prances out from stage left.)

TUKIMO: Wow! That is an incredible horse!

MAKI: You bet. He's magic, too. You can ride him up the mountain, ride him back down, smooth as silk. Third gear all the way.

TUKIMO: You're really going to let me ride him?

MAKI: Why not? You're a nice guy, and nice guys deserve to finish first once in awhile. Oh, you better take these.

(MAKI hands TUKIMO a pair of silver sneakers.)

TUKIMO: Diamond horseshoes?

MAKI: Put them on the horse, and he'll never slip. Oh, and if you're going to meet the Boss' Beautiful Daughter, you better dress a little snappier. *(puts a fancy jacket on TUKIMO and hands him a pair of white gloves)* Saddle up!

(TUKIMO rides HEIKKI to the glass mountain, where GUARDS, DAUGHTER'S GIRLFRIENDS and DAUGHTER all are asleep. He and HEIKKI easily climb the mountain, and TUKIMO nudges the DAUGHTER awake.)

DAUGHTER: What are you doing here?

TUKIMO: I rode up the glass mountain.

DAUGHTER: Rode up the glass mountain? You? Just like that?

TUKIMO: I came to see you. You're the Boss' Beautiful Daughter, aren't you?

DAUGHTER: Well, that's kind of a superficial way to characterize some-body. I mean, unless you're talking about my inner beauty.

TUKIMO: Oh, I am. And I've heard you're really intelligent and tal-ented, too.

DAUGHTER: Well, I'm glad *somebody* thinks so. You don't know how grotty it's been to sit up here day after day after day and watch these complete imbeciles try and climb this stupid glass mountain my par-ents built just so they could get me out of the house. Like I have nothing else to do with my life but wait around to get married!

TUKIMO: Well, this *is* a folktale. Hey, do you want to see my magic horse?

(He offers her his hand and helps her down off mountain; they stand next to HEIKKI, admiring him.)

DAUGHTER: He's really cool! Can we ride him to a shop or something?

(DAUGHTER, TUKIMO and HEIKKI ride off left, exit; a NEWS-BOY enters from stage right, hawking papers.)

NEWSBOY: Extra! Extra! Read all about it! Suitor Found for Boss' Daughter! Read all about it!

(Entire cast [except for MAKI and HEIKKI] gathers in front of glass mountain; TUKIMO is dressed in ragged overalls.)

BOSS: Well, well, daughter—who is the plucky, I mean, lucky fellow?
DAUGHTER: I don't know.
BOSS' WIFE: You don't know?
DAUGHTER: In all the excitement, I forgot to ask his name. *(sighs)* And we had such a great time at the mall.

(KUSTA swaggers forward.)

KUSTA: Uh, sir? I cannot tell a lie. It was me who climbed the mountain.

(KALAMI swaggers forward.)

KALAMI: No way, bro'…it was me!
DAUGHTER: Well, then which of you has the golden apple?

(KUSTA and KALAMI exchange nervous glances.)

KUSTA: Uhhhhhh…I had the apple…but my dog ate it.
KALAMI: No, really, *I* had the apple, and *his* dog ate it!
BOSS: Guards! Get these two clowns away from here.

(GUARDS grab KUSTA and KALAMI; DAUGHTER spies TUKIMO at the edge of the stage.)

BOSS' WIFE: Oh, this is senseless! Daughter, how can we announce your marriage if you don't know who it is you're marrying?
DAUGHTER: Who is that boy?
KUSTA: That goofball? He's our little brother, Tukimo.
DAUGHTER: That's him! Mama, Papa, that's the boy who climbed the mountain last night!
KALAMI: You're mental! Cinders never goes anywhere!

(TUKIMO comes forward to center stage, takes the DAUGHTER'S hand.)

TUKIMO: Last night, I wore clothes of pure silk and rode a magic horse to the top of a glass mountain.

KUSTA: Liar!

TUKIMO: And I met the most beautiful girl in the whole county—the Boss' Daughter.

KALAMI: I'm sorry, your bossness—the dude is, like, gonzo.

BOSS: Cinders, Tukimo, whatever your name is—we do not take lightly to mockery. You claim to have climbed the glass mountain—a feat of bravery and skill no stalwart swell or daring dandy in this entire county has accomplished. Where is your proof?

TUKIMO: Proof? Oh, you mean this? *(pulls out golden apple, gives it to BOSS)*

(Everyone gasps.)

KUSTA: He stole that apple from me!

KALAMI: He's always making up stories and stuff.

DAUGHTER: Wait! *I* know the identity of the boy who climbed the mountain last night. When I gave him the apple, I carved a message into the skin.

(She takes the apple from Boss, points to it and reads:)

DAUGHTER: "To a really magical guy. See you later, alligator!" *(takes TUKIMO'S arm)* Mama, Papa—this is the man I'm going to marry!

(The crowd cheers [except for KUSTA and KALAMI] and congratulates TUKIMO and the BOSS' DAUGHTER, who dash offstage left followed by the happy crowd, KUSTA and KALAMI at the end being prodded by the GUARDS. NARRATOR stands and addresses audience.)

NARRATOR: And so, because he listened to his dream, the poor working boy Tukimo married the Boss' Beautiful Daughter. The boss became very fond of Tukimo and put him in charge of all his business. Tukimo became very wealthy and, of course, he and his beautiful bride lived happily ever after—though they did start spending the winters in Miami to get away from all that Michigan snow. *(He starts to exit right, then turns.)* Oh, and those nasty brothers? They ended up working for the big boss, too. They got to work in the furnace room…shoveling cinders. *(exits)*

(LIGHTS OUT.)

THE END

THE HONEST MILLER
El Molinero Honesto

The Honest Miller comes from the folklore of Mexican-Americans living in the Southwestern United States. It incorporates elements from many tales known around the world: two men wagering on the honesty of another, a valuable item discovered in a fish, lost treasure found by the hand that hid it, an honest man subjected to many trials before achieving final vindication and reward. All add up to an exciting, colorful drama.

TIME: Mid-1800s

PLACE: A small village in New Mexico

CAST: Narrator *(Narrator lines can be given to more than one actor.)*

Hawk	Pedro
Grocer	Antonio
Clayseller	Miller
Fisherman	Miller's Wife
Fisherman's Wife	Miller's 3 Children
Jeweler	Servant #1
Jeweler's Wife	Servant #2

STAGE SET: adobe walls; a table and a chair; a mill stone; a tree

PROPS: peso notes (play money of any kind); handkerchief; small leather or cloth bag; earthen jar; box of white clay; piece of lead; diamond; frying pan; bucket; fancy serving dishes, bird's nest

COSTUMES: Everyone except Pedro and Antonio can dress in simple, loose-fitting 19th-century Mexican peasant clothes: blousy shirts, baggy pants, sandals, straw sombreros for men, head scarves for women; the Jeweler and Jeweler's Wife may have additional accessories befitting their greater wealth; Pedro and Antonio dress as young dandies: vests, riding boots, colorful jackets and fancy sombreros

(LIGHTS UP FULL; at stage right NARRATOR sits on a low wall. He greets the audience:)

NARRATOR: *¡Buenas dias, muchachas y muchachos!* Good day, girls and boys! Once upon a time in New Mexico, a little more than a hundred years ago, there were two friends, whose names were Pedro and Antonio.

(PEDRO and ANTONIO enter as introduced, PEDRO from stage left, ANTONIO from stage right; they notice each other and cross to center to shake hands in front of table.)

PEDRO: *¡Antonio, mi amigo!* My friend!

ANTONIO: *¡Buenas dias, Pedro! ¿Que pasa, hombre?* What's happening, man?

(PEDRO offers the chair to ANTONIO, who sits; they both pull out big wads of peso bills from their pockets, showing them to each other and waving them about.)

NARRATOR: Pedro and Antonio were very good friends. They were also very wealthy, and they enjoyed talking a lot about money. They talked about their money, about other people's money; anything to do with money, they would talk about—endlessly. One day, they got into a big argument.

PEDRO: Listen, Antonio, to what I am saying. If you already have money, it is easy to get rich. If you don't have money, you stay poor.

ANTONIO: No, Pedro. It isn't money that makes a man rich; it is *suerte*—luck. With the right kind of luck, even the poorest man can become rich.

PEDRO: Antonio, my friend, you are *loco*—crazy! No one who is really, really poor can ever become really, really rich...unless they are also dishonest. Luck has nothing to do with it!

ANTONIO: Very well, amigo. Let us put our beliefs to a test. We will find an honest man who is poor—

PEDRO: And see if it is luck—

ANTONIO: Or money—

PEDRO: That makes him rich.

(PEDRO and ANTONIO shake hands; LIGHTS DIM, THEN UP FULL as PEDRO and ANTONIO meander around stage, finally coming to within a few feet of A MILLER, who stands stage left grinding on a mill stone.)

NARRATOR: The two friends walked throughout the countryside for several days. Finally, they came to a small village where they saw a Miller hard at work, busily grinding corn and wheat.

PEDRO: Look, Antonio: *un molinero.* A miller! *Buenas tardes, señor.*

MILLER: Good afternoon to you, too, señores. How can I help you today?

ANTONIO: Tell us how do you operate your milling business?

MILLER: My business? It is not my business, but the business of the man for whom I work.

PEDRO: I see. How much do you earn for your work?

MILLER: I earn four bits a day. And with that I support a wife and three children.

ANTONIO: Four bits a day? You mean to say that you can support a family of five on only fifteen pesos a month?

MILLER: We live very modestly, señores. We have enough food and clothing. We have our good health. There is nothing important we lack.

(PEDRO and ANTONIO turn away from the MILLER and whisper to each other; PEDRO pulls out a wad of bills from his pocket and gives it to an astonished MILLER.)

PEDRO: Amigo, I am going to give you two thousand pesos. You may do whatever you want with the money.

MILLER: Two thousand pesos! *¡Gracias!* Thank you! But why? Why do you give me this money, when you have just met me?

PEDRO: My friend and I have an argument. He contends that it is luck which makes a man prosperous; I believe it is money.

ANTONIO: By giving you this money, perhaps we can settle our argument. Take it and do what you want with it.

(PEDRO and ANTONIO exit left; the MILLER stares at the money.)

NARRATOR: So the poor Miller took the money. He spent the rest of the day thinking about these two strange men and about the money they had given him—more money than he ever seen in his entire life. What could he possibly do with it all?

MILLER: Ah-ha! I will buy food for my family. I will take ten pesos and wrap the rest of the money in a handkerchief. I will put the handkerchief in my bag and go to the market.

(GROCER enters from right, stands at center by table; the MILLER goes to him and hands him money.)

GROCER: That will be ten pesos for the groceries, señor. And here is an excellent piece of meat for your family.

(GROCER hands MILLER a wrapped package, which the MILLER puts in his bag.)

MILLER: *Gracias, señor.* Thank you so much.

(GROCER exits right; MILLER walks slowly left; A HAWK slinks out from stage right, sees the MILLER and begins to stalk him, flapping its wings.)

NARRATOR: But on the way home, the Miller was attacked by a hawk that had smelled the meat in his bag. The Miller tried to fight off the bird, but the hawk grabbed the bag and flew away.

(HAWK exits left.)

MILLER: *¡Soy tres tonto!* I am so stupid! It would have been better to let that hungry bird have the meat. I should have gone straight home, and this wouldn't have happened. Alas, I am as poor tonight as I was this morning. But what if I meet those two men, and they ask me what I did with the money? They will say I am a thief!

(MILLER walks wearily back to his mill stone.)

NARRATOR: The next morning the Miller got up and went to work as usual, and it wasn't long before he forgot about the two men and the money.

(PEDRO and ANTONIO enter from left.)

NARRATOR: But three months later, the two men were back again.

PEDRO: *(to ANTONIO)* ¡Mira! Look! It is our friend, the Miller.

ANTONIO: Señor! You are still working at the mill stone. We thought by now you would be fabulously wealthy with the money we gave you.

MILLER: *(bows)* Señores, I am so ashamed. I know you will not believe me, but after I saw you that day, I was on my way home with your two thousand pesos wrapped in a bag. Suddenly, from the sky, a hawk swooped down, grabbed the bag and flew away. It is the truth.

PEDRO: A hawk? *(chuckles)*

ANTONIO: Flew away with the money? *(chuckles)* Why, that is the most ridiculous thing I've ever heard! Wouldn't you say so, Pedro? *(laughs)*

PEDRO: Si, si, Antonio. That is truly the silliest story I have ever heard in my entire life. *(laughs heartily, then pulls out a wad of bills from his pocket and gives it to the MILLER)* Here, my good man. Have another two thousand pesos and let's try again.

MILLER: *(falls to his knees)* Señores! I am overwhelmed with your generosity! But perhaps you should give this money to someone else. I…I am not worthy.

PEDRO: Nonsense, Miller. We want to give it to *you* because we believe you are an honest man.

ANTONIO: Besides, if my friend and I are to settle our argument, you *must* take the money.

(PEDRO and ANTONIO exit left. THE MILLER counts the money, stuffs it inside his shirt and walks toward center stage.)

NARRATOR: As soon as the men left, the Miller thought about what to do so he wouldn't lose the money again. He decided to head straight home.

(MILLER stops at table and looks around, confused.)

MILLER: Maria! Maria! Maria, I am home! I have a big surprise!

NARRATOR: But his wife was not home, nor were his children. He didn't know what to do with the money. But then he saw the jar where his wife kept bran.

MILLER: Ah-ha! This is as safe a place as anywhere. I will put this bundle of money into the bottom of this jar…spread the bran over it like so...*bueno!* (*yawns*) It is time for a siesta. (*sits in chair, puts his head on the table*) Maria will be so surprised when I tell her about our good fortune...

(*LIGHTS DIM, THEN COME UP SLOWLY as the MILLER'S WIFE enters from right with the CLAYSELLER, who carries a box of white clay. She points to a spot next to the jar, and the CLAYSELLER lays down the box. He picks up the jar, bows and exits right. THE MILLER'S WIFE takes a handful of clay and splats it on the table, waking the MILLER.*)

MILLER: Maria! I had the most wonderful dream...no, wait, it was not a dream...it is true!

MILLER'S WIFE: What is it, my husband?

MILLER: Three months ago two men I had never seen before gave me two thousand pesos. They told me to spend it any way I wanted. But before I could spend the money, I lost it.

MILLER'S WIFE: Oh, husband, that is very, very bad.

MILLER: But today they came again, and they gave me another two thousand pesos!

MILLER'S WIFE: Now that is very, very good! I wish *I* had dreams like that.

MILLER: But it's true! It's true, I tell you!

MILLER'S WIFE: Of course it is, husband. I believe you. Look at this beautiful clay I just bought. I think we have enough to whitewash the entire house.

MILLER: That's nice. We need to whitewash the house very much. (*pause*) Maria...how did you buy the clay if we have no money?

MILLER'S WIFE: The clayseller said he would trade for something of value. And the only thing we had of value was that old jar full of bran. So I traded it for the clay.

MILLER: (*stands*) No!

MILLER'S WIFE: Yes! See for yourself!

(*THE MILLER turns and stares at the empty spot where the jar had been; he groans and beats his head with his fists.*)

MILLER: No, no, no, no, no!

MILLER'S WIFE: Why, husband! Don't you like the color of the clay?

MILLER: The money those men gave me today—

MILLER'S WIFE: Yes—

MILLER: I hid it in the bottom of that jar—the same jar you have traded for dirt! Oh, we are ruined! We are ruined! What will I tell the men? They will think I am a liar and a thief for sure!

MILLER'S WIFE: *(comforts him)* Now, now, husband. Let them think what they want. We have in our lives only what we are meant to have. It is our lot to be poor until God wills it otherwise.

(She exits right; the MILLER returns slowly to his mill stone.)

NARRATOR: The Miller was consoled and went back to work the next day. Time came and went until, sure enough, one day the two wealthy friends came to see him and inquire about the money.

(PEDRO and ANTONIO enter from left; they talk with the MILLER.)

NARRATOR: Once again, the Miller was truthful and told them what had happened to the second two thousand pesos.

PEDRO: I don't know, Antonio…I find this man's wild stories hard to believe. I think he gambled the money and lost it. But I still think it is money and not luck that makes a man prosper.

ANTONIO: Well, you certainly didn't prove your point by giving money to this miserable wretch. Good day, you luckless man.

MILLER: *(bows)* Gracias, señores. *Vaya con dios.* May you go with God.

(PEDRO and ANTONIO move to exit left, but ANTONIO stops and takes a piece of lead from his pocket.)

ANTONIO: Say there, Miller. Here is a worthless piece of lead I've been carrying around awhile. *(tosses it to him)* Maybe you can use it for something.

(PEDRO and ANTONIO exit; the MILLER studies the lead and sighs; he starts to throw it away but puts it in his pocket instead; he walks to center stage and wearily sits at table.)

NARRATOR: The Miller went home to his family and ate dinner and got ready for bed. Around midnight, he heard a knock on the door.

(THE FISHERMAN'S WIFE enters from right, knocks.)

FISHERMAN'S WIFE: It's me, your neighbor! The Fisherman's Wife. My husband is going fishing tomorrow, and he wants to know if you have any lead you can spare.

MILLER: Lead? Why would I have lead? I am a miller not a miner.

FISHERMAN'S WIFE: He needs the lead to weigh down his nets. Do you have any to spare?

MILLER: Can't you hear me, I said—*(feels the piece of lead in his pocket)* I said…yes, of course, I have some lead. You may have it.

FISHERMAN'S WIFE: *(takes it from him) Gracias, señor, gracias.* I promise that the first fish my husband catches, he will give to you.

(The MILLER lays his head on the table.)

NARRATOR: The Miller went back to sleep, and the next day he went to work as always. But that night, when he came home, he found his wife cooking a big fish for supper.

(MILLER'S WIFE enters from right with frying pan, serves fish to MILLER.)

MILLER: Since when are we so wealthy we can afford fresh fish for supper?

MILLER'S WIFE: Don't you remember our neighbor promised us the first fish her husband caught? This is it, and it's ours. But you know, you should have been here when I cleaned the fish. I found a large piece of glass in his stomach.

MILLER: Glass? What did you do with it?

MILLER'S WIFE: I gave it to the children to play with.

(THREE CHILDREN enter from right, scampering and shouting, playing keepaway from each other with the piece of glass.)

CHILD #1: Mine! Mine! *(taunts CHILD #2 with glass)*

CHILD #2: No, it isn't! Give it here!

CHILD #3: Here! Here! Throw it here!

MILLER: ¡Silencio! Quiet! At once!

MILLER'S WIFE: Children! Please, stop quarreling over that bauble!

(The JEWELER'S WIFE enters from left, knocks on door.)

JEWELER'S WIFE: Hello! It is your neighbor, the Jeweler's Wife. There is an awful lot of noise in there, and it is very late. Can't you make those children be quiet?

(MILLER'S WIFE shoos CHILDREN away and opens the door for the JEWELER'S WIFE; CHILDREN exit right and the one who has the piece of glass drops it on the ground before exiting.)

MILLER'S WIFE: I am sorry, señora. Our children get so excited by the smallest toy. *(picks up glass)* Look…just a silly piece of broken glass.

JEWELER'S WIFE: Broken glass? Really? Do you mind if I…take a look?

MILLER'S WIFE: Of course. *(shows glass)*

JEWELER'S WIFE: This *is* a pretty piece of glass, isn't it? You know, I have a piece at home just like it. Would you let me show this to my husband?

MILLER: Sure, go ahead. It's just glass.

(JEWELER'S WIFE dashes off left to her husband, the JEWELER, and excitedly shows him the glass, which he studies intently)

JEWELER: It is a diamond!

JEWELER'S WIFE: I thought so. What shall we do?

JEWELER: Tell the neighbors we'll give them fifty pesos for it. But don't tell them it's a diamond.

JEWELER'S WIFE: Of course not.

(JEWELER'S WIFE runs back to the MILLER and MILLER'S WIFE with the glass.)

JEWELER'S WIFE: Yes, we have one exactly like this. My husband is willing to buy it from you for, say, fifty pesos. Just so we can have a pair, you know.

(The MILLER'S WIFE goes to the MILLER and whispers in his ear.)

MILLER: Fifty pesos! Why would they offer fifty pesos for a worthless piece of glass?

JEWELER'S WIFE: What do you say, neighbor? Fifty pesos for the little piece of glass?

MILLER: That is not enough. Offer more.

JEWELER'S WIFE: More? Well, maybe a little. How about sixty pesos?

MILLER: No.

JEWELER'S WIFE: Seventy pesos.

MILLER: No.

JEWELER'S WIFE: Seventy-five?

MILLER: Not enough.

JEWELER'S WIFE: *(frantic)* All right. Fifty thousand pesos! I'll give you fifty thousand pesos, but I must have that glass!

MILLER: Are you mad?

(JEWELER bursts in with a bucket of pesos.)

JEWELER: She *is* mad! I'll give you one hundred thousand pesos!

MILLER'S WIFE: Sold!

(MILLER'S WIFE grabs glass from her husband and puts it in JEWELER'S hand; grabs cash from Jeweler and puts it in her husband's hand; she then shakes hands with her husband and the JEWELER; JEWELER and JEWELER'S WIFE exit left.)

MILLER'S WIFE: Husband, what are we going to do with this money?

MILLER: I think…I think I will start my own mill. And then we will see if our luck changes.

(They exit right; LIGHTS DIM.)

NARRATOR: Indeed, the Miller's luck did change. He set up his own mill, and he grew very rich. Within just a couple of years, he had a new home for his family, and his wife and children had every luxury they could want. Then one day, he saw Pedro and Antonio riding by. He stopped them and told them of his success; then he took them out to his new house in the country.

(LIGHTS UP FULL ON CENTER STAGE where the table is topped by a beautiful cloth; the MILLER is dressed in fine clothes; his wife, also dressed richly, stands alongside him as he talks to PEDRO and ANTONIO; SERVANT #1 places serving dishes filled with food on the table.)

PEDRO: You still tell the wildest stories, señor. A diamond inside a fish…really!

MILLER: Gentlemen, I tell you the truth. But come, let us eat before we talk anymore.

(CHILDREN #1 AND #2 run in from left.)

CHILD #1: Poppa, poppa! Come look at the tree outside!
CHILD #2: It is the nest of a bird! A hawk!

(All rush left to the tree where CHILD #3 stands, pointing upward.)

CHILD #3: Up there! In the high branches!
PEDRO: Why, the children are absolutely correct. It *is* the nest of a hawk.
ANTONIO: I've never seen such a nest. I would like to take a closer look.
MILLER: Of course! *(to servant)* Gregorio, bring us that nest, *por favor.*
SERVANT #1: Yes, master. *(exits left, returns in a moment holding a nest)*
MILLER: Here. Let's see what we have. *(lays nest on ground, digs inside it and pulls out a dirty old bag)* ¡Mira! This is the same bag in which I put the first two thousand pesos you gave me!
PEDRO: If this is the same bag, then the money should still be there.
NARRATOR: And sure enough, when they unfolded the bag, they found the money—minus the ten pesos the Miller had spent on the piece of meat. But still, not everyone was completely satisfied.
ANTONIO: I wonder what *really* happened to the second two thousand pesos we gave you.

(SERVANT #2 runs in from right, carrying the earthen jar and a rag-covered package.)

SERVANT #2: Señor Molinero! Look at what I found inside this jar!
MILLER: *(takes jar, examines it)* Where did you get this?
SERVANT #2: I was feeding your horses and realized I had run out of grain. So I went to the neighbor and was able to buy this jar of bran. When I emptied the jar, this package fell out.
PEDRO: Let me see that. *(unwraps the cloth and pulls out peso notes)* Incredible!
MILLER: The second two thousand pesos you gave me! So you see, I am an honest man after all.
ANTONIO: And at this point, a very rich one.
PEDRO: But that still doesn't settle our question, Antonio.
ANTONIO: Was it luck—

PEDRO: Or money—

ANTONIO: That made this honest man rich?

MILLER: *(puts his arms around PEDRO and ANTONIO)* I think, my friends, you will have to agree…it was a little bit of both.

(They all laugh; LIGHTS OUT.)

THE END

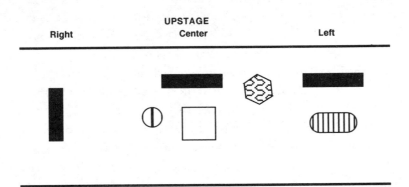

UPSTAGE

Right   Center   Left

Stage Plan *The Honest Miller*

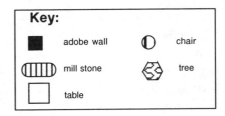

Key:

■	adobe wall	◐	chair
⬭	mill stone	⬡	tree
☐	table		

SHLEMAZL GOES TO PARADISE

Shlemazl Goes to Paradise is based on a tale from the rich folklore heritage of Eastern European Jews. The name of the lead character comes from two words in the Yiddish language—*shlimm* ("bad") and *mazel* ("luck")—an apt description of a man who thinks the grass is always greener on the other side of the fence but isn't ever quite sure which side of the fence he's actually standing on! As an old Yiddish proverb says, "Nor naronim far-lozen zich oif nisim"—only fools rely on miracles.

TIME: Now and Forever

PLACE: A small village in the country

CAST:
Tumler	Mrs. Plosher
Shlemazl	Kishke the Butcher
Shlemazl's Wife	Blintz the Baker
Shlemazl's 4 Children	Rabbi Shofar
Mayor Farmisht	2 Maleks

STAGE SET: kitchen table and 2 chairs; 4 stools

PROPS: violin; knapsack; measuring cup; broom; potato peeler; potatoes in bowl; a pair of beat-up shoes; butcher knife; sharpening stone; rolling pin; bread dough; scroll; pig mask

COSTUMES: late 19th-century Eastern European peasant dress for all characters: Rabbi Shofar is dressed in rabbinical garb, Mayor Farmisht would wear a frock coat, Tumler can wear a derby or other carnival barker accessories, the 2 Maleks might wear a beany with a propeller to denote their otherworldly origin

(LIGHTS UP. At stage right TUMLER stands, playing a violin—badly. He stops and speaks to audience.)

TUMLER: Say, did you hear about the guy with such bad luck his mail arrives "postage due"? Or the time he was shipwrecked on a desert island all alone with one beautiful girl: his sister. Well, I knew a guy like that. He lived in my village, and his name was Shlemazl. Look, there he is now!

(SHLEMAZL enters from right, head hung down and muttering, and shuffles past TUMLER. TUMLER greets him, but SHLEMAZL just keeps walking to center stage where he stops in front of a kitchen table.)

TUMLER: Shlemazl! It is your friend, Tumler. How are you today? *(to audience)* Poor fellow! If he sold umbrellas, it would never rain. If he sold lightbulbs, it would never get dark. But one day, my friend Shlemazl had a piece of good luck: he discovered Paradise.

(TUMLER plays a few notes on the violin, exits right; SHLEMAZL'S WIFE and FOUR SHLEMAZL CHILDREN scurry onstage from left, nattering noisily, and congregate around SHLEMAZL at center stage.)

SHLEMAZL'S WIFE: Husband! Husband! These kinder are driving me crazy! Did you find a job today?

SHLEMAZL: Job-schmob! I can't even think with all his racket! Everybody be quiet!

(CHILDREN stop talking and sit down on floor, sobbing.)

SHLEMAZL'S WIFE: Some husband you are! Look at this tiny house. We have barely enough money to buy food, and all you can say is, "Everybody be quiet!" Here! *(she thrusts a broom into his hands)* Try and make yourself useful.

(She sits down at table and starts peeling potatoes; children jump up and run offstage left, shouting; SHLEMAZL sweeps sluggishly and addresses audience.)

SHLEMAZL: Talking to her is like talking to the wall. Only the wall doesn't talk back! Ever since the day we were married, it's "Shlemazl do this, Shlemazl do that!" It never stops! But someday…someday, I will find Paradise.

(MRS. PLOSHER enters from stage left bearing a measuring cup and calls out to him.)

MRS. PLOSHER: Shlemazl! It's so good to see you. And here you are, hard at work. I don't understand why your wife says you're a lazy no-goodnik.

SHLEMAZL: *(sighs)* Good morning, Mrs. Plosher. How are you today?

MRS. PLOSHER: Don't ask! I'm out of matzo again, and my health is so bad, I'm beside myself. My back is killing me, my stomach is churning like a steamship, my eyes are so sore, I can barely hold them open. Oh, and my arthritis! It's absolutely killing me. And when I went to the doctor, he wanted to charge me forty dollars for looking at my ingrown toenail. "Doctor," I said, "For forty dollars I could have a broken leg!" You know, Shlemazl, when I came over I had a terrible headache. Now it's gone! Isn't that a miracle?

SHLEMAZL: No, Mrs. Plosher, your headache isn't gone. You've given it to me!

(MRS. PLOSHER huffs and exits left; SHLEMAZL drops the broom on the floor.)

SHLEMAZL: Enough already! I'm going to Paradise today!

(SHLEMAZL goes to kitchen table and picks up a knapsack underneath it. SOUND CUE: TUMLER plays violin to dialogue.)

SHLEMAZL: Don't bother getting up. I'm leaving.

SHLEMAZL'S WIFE: And where do you think you're going?

SHLEMAZL: I am going to Paradise!

SHLEMAZL'S WIFE: Mazel tov! *(waves goodbye and resumes peeling potatoes)*

(SOUND CUE: TUMLER plays violin. SHLEMAZL walks left then right and passes in front of TUMLER, who puts down his violin.)

TUMLER: My good friend, Shlemazl! Where are you going in such a hurry?

SHLEMAZL: Tumler, I am going to find Paradise!

TUMLER: Paradise? Shlemazl, have you ever been to Paradise?

SHLEMAZL: No, but I know it's that way. *(points left)* Or is it maybe this way? *(points right)*

(TUMLER picks up a pair of beat-up, old shoes from behind him and hands them to SHLEMAZL.)

TUMLER: My friend, put on these shoes.

SHLEMAZL: But I already have shoes. See?

TUMLER: Shoes like this, you don't have. These are magic shoes.

SHLEMAZL: They look like they were made a hundred years ago! Why there's hardly any leather left at all!

TUMLER: Not much leather, but plenty magic. Whichever way they point, you must follow them.

SHLEMAZL: And they'll lead me to Paradise?

TUMLER: Straight to the gate. All you have to do is walk.

(SHLEMAZL takes his shoes off and puts on the shoes TUMLER gave him; they shake hands and SHLEMAZL walks toward center stage, carrying his shoes and knapsack.)

SHLEMAZL: I'm on my way to Paradise! *(waves)*

TUMLER: Send a postcard when you get there.

(KISHKE THE BUTCHER, BLINTZ THE BAKER, MAYOR FARMISHT and RABBI SHOFAR enter from left and sit on stools facing audience. SPOTLIGHT ON KISHKE.)

SHLEMAZL: *(tramps around stage)* Here I am, leaving this little village for the last time. Oh, there is Kishke the Butcher. Goodbye, Kishke! Goodbye!

KISHKE: *(sharpening a butcher knife on a stone)* Goodbye? I am not going anywhere.

SHLEMAZL: Oh, but I am! I am going to Paradise! Where I won't have to buy any more of your spoiled, overpriced meat.

KISHKE: I should be so lucky. Have a good trip!

(SPOTLIGHT OFF ON KISHKE; SPOTLIGHT ON BLINTZ. SHLEMAZL walks around, stops in front of BLINTZ THE BAKER, who is kneading dough with a rolling pin.)

SHLEMAZL: Blintz! I'm off to Paradise!

BLINTZ: How about taking a few bagels with you?

SHLEMAZL: Blintz, your bagels are so tough, all the cream cheese in the world wouldn't make them edible!

BLINTZ: So, don't eat—use them as doorstops for your new house in Paradise.

(SHLEMAZL waves his hand in disgust and walks away; SPOT-LIGHT OFF ON BLINTZ; SPOTLIGHT ON MAYOR FARM-ISHT.)

MAYOR FARMISHT: Citizen Shlemazl!

SHLEMAZL: So long, Mayor Farmisht!

MAYOR FARMISHT: Wait! *(runs to SHLEMAZL and vigorously shakes his hand)* As your Mayor, I'm asking for your vote in Tuesday's election.

SHLEMAZL: My vote? *(hands his old shoes to the MAYOR)* You're welcome to it, Mayor. I won't need it anymore. I'm going to Paradise.

MAYOR FARMISHT: Thank you, thank you! Oh, when you get to Paradise, can you send a small campaign contribution?

(SHLEMAZL shakes his head and walks away. SPOTLIGHT OFF ON MAYOR; SPOTLIGHT ON RABBI. Shlemazl approaches RABBI SHOFAR, who sits reading a scroll.)

SHLEMAZL: Rabbi Shofar! I am the luckiest man in the world!

RABBI SHOFAR: Lucky? The unluckiest man in the world is the man who does not know how lucky he is.

SHLEMAZL: You don't understand, Rabbi. I am through with this ridiculous village and everyone in it. Today, I am off to Paradise!

RABBI SHOFAR: The man who can't dance says it's the fiddler who can't keep time.

SHLEMAZL: Rabbi, I think you're jealous because I'm going to Paradise, and you're not.

RABBI SHOFAR: And if my grandmother had wheels, she'd be a wagon. Have a good time in Paradise, Shlemazl.

SHLEMAZL: Believe me, Rabbi, I will!

(SPOTLIGHT OFF ON RABBI. SHLEMAZL walks around stage, stops at down left and looks offstage into audience.)

TUMLER: With that, Shlemazl walked out of the village and came to a big hill, which he climbed. At the top of the hill, he peered into the valley below and looked for the last time at his village. He was quite certain he would never see it again.

(SHLEMAZL shrugs and walks in place.)

TUMLER: At the top of the hill was a forest, and into this forest Shlemazl walked. And walked. And walked…until it was almost dark, and he decided to rest for the night—absolutely positive he would reach Paradise in the morning.

(SHLEMAZL stops walking and lies down, head on knapsack; he takes off his shoes and places them above his head, pointing to stage left.)

TUMLER: And before he went to sleep, he took off his magic shoes and pointed them straight toward Paradise.

(TUMLER plays a lullaby on the violin, then stops as TWO MALEKS enter stealthily from stage right, urging each other to be quiet and not awake the sleeping SHLEMAZL.)

TUMLER: Well, Shlemazl didn't know it, but he had some invisible traveling companions—a pair of Maleks. What is a Malek, you ask? Some people say they are angels, others say they are—well, a bit too full of mischief to be genuine angels. Every human being journeys through life with two Maleks by his side, guiding him to his true destiny. Shlemazl, of course, thought Maleks were just make-believe, a notion his own personal Maleks found very amusing.

MALEK #1: Look at him…sleeping like a baby.

MALEK #2: He should. He thinks like a baby. Paradise? He wouldn't know Paradise if it turned him upside down and threw a cherry pie in his face.

MALEK #1: So? We should help him, maybe, find this Paradise he looks for so hard.

MALEK #2: Okay by me. Let's start with those shoes.

MALEK #1: Those shoes by his noggin?

MALEK #2: He thinks they're pointing toward Paradise.

MALEK #1: He's crazy! Paradise is that way. *(points to stage right)*

MALEK #2: Where we just came from?

MALEK #1: Sure. Didn't we just come from there?

MALEK #2: Of course we did.

MALEK #1: And we know the way to Paradise, right?

MALEK #2: Of course we do. We were born there.

MALEK #1: Well then. If you ask me, this fellow is all turned around.

MALEK #2: That is truly a shame. As his own personal Maleks, we should take pity.

MALEK #1: Show mercy.

MALEK #2: Give him a hand.

MALEK #1: Cut him a break.

(MALEK #1 picks up the shoes and turns them so they face the opposite direction—stage right.)

MALEK #2: It would be the friendly thing to do.

MALEK #1: The neighborly thing to do.

MALEK #2: Kind.

MALEK #1: Sociable.

MALEK #2: Fitting and just.

MALEK #1: As in desserts!

MALEK #2: Last one to Paradise is a rotten egg!

(The TWO MALEKS snicker and tiptoe offstage, exiting left. SOUND CUE: TUMLER plays violin until Shlemazl wakes with a start, jumps up and stretches and yawns loudly.)

TUMLER: When Shlemazl awoke the next morning, he was so excited, he was ready to bust.

SHLEMAZL: Today, I reach Paradise! Let's see, where are those magic shoes? Ah, here they are!

(He puts on shoes and begins walking in place, facing audience.)

SHLEMAZL: Finally, I'm through the forest! *(peers ahead)* And look! There is a hilltop. Paradise must be in the valley below! *(He jogs in place faster, then stops, frowning.)* That's strange. It seems so…small. Not much bigger than my own village. Hmmm…I was sure Paradise would be a very big place. Hmmm. It does have a synagogue. And a town hall. A bakery and a butcher shop. Just like my old village—

how convenient! Oh well, I'll just go down the hill…and I'll be in Paradise!

(He turns and walks in circles for a few seconds, then moves behind upstage, stopping in front of the stool on which RABBI SHOFAR sits, reading a scroll. SPOTLIGHT ON RABBI.)

SHLEMAZL: How peculiar. The synagogue in Paradise seems oddly familiar. Hmmm…and the rabbi looks like my old rabbi.

RABBI SHOFAR: Old? Who're you calling old? You're no spring tomato yourself, boychick!

(SHLEMAZL backs away to MAYOR'S stool. SPOTLIGHT OFF RABBI; SPOTLIGHT ON MAYOR.)

MAYOR FARMISHT: *(hands out, pleading)* If you lend me your vote on Tuesday, I will gladly repay you on Thursday.

SHLEMAZL: *(turns away to audience)* I never knew Mayor Farmisht had a twin brother.

(SHLEMAZL moves to BLINTZ'S stool. SPOTLIGHT OFF MAYOR; SPOTLIGHT ON BLINTZ.)

BLINTZ: Bagels! Get your red-hot bagels! Here you go, my good man: try this fresh, tasty morsel! *(hands bagel to SHLEMAZL)*

SHLEMAZL: Looks just like Blintz the Baker. But that's impossible! *(bites into bagel, grimaces, hands bagel back to BLINTZ)* Yeck! Tastes just like Blintz the Baker.

(SPOTLIGHT OFF BLINTZ; SPOTLIGHT ON KISHKE. SHLE-MAZL wanders dazedly around stage, then stops as KISHKE sings to melody of Popeye the Sailor Man.*)*

KISHKE: *(sings)*
I'm Kishke the Butcher Man, I'm Kishke the Butcher Man
I chop up the herring with skill and with daring
I'm Kishke the Butcher Man

(SPOTLIGHT OFF KISHKE.)

SHLEMAZL: *(shakes his head)* Ai-yi-yi! I must be dreaming. If this is Paradise…then pigs can talk.

(MRS. PLOSHER enters from left, a pig mask on her head, and quickly crosses stage in front of the astonished SHLEMAZL to exit right.)

MRS. PLOSHER: Don't ask! My husband says, "Darling, it's the best thing for a cold." "Better than chicken soup," I ask? "Try it," he says, "it'll grow on you." It did! *(exits)*

(SPOTLIGHT ON KITCHEN TABLE, where SHLEMAZL'S wife sits, peeling potatoes.)

SHLEMAZL: *(points at wife)* If I didn't know better, I would almost believe that was my house.

SHLEMAZL'S WIFE: *(looks up)* There you are! Loafing around town again the whole night and day. Supper's almost ready. Better come in and make yourself useful.

SHLEMAZL: *(laughs)* Ha-ha-ha! *(to audience)* This woman is cuckoo! She thinks she knows me! Can you imagine the poor shnook who's married to her?

(SHLEMAZL'S FOUR CHILDREN skip onstage from left and congregate around him.)

CHILD #1: Look, father has come home!

SHLEMAZL: *(to audience)* These look very much like my own children.

CHILD #2: Daddy, daddy, we missed you!

SHLEMAZL: How can you miss me when I only came here to Paradise this morning?

CHILD #3: Please say you won't go away again!

SHLEMAZL: Go away? Sonny, I just got here!

CHILD #4: *(leads SHLEMAZL to chair)* Sit down at the table and tell us all about Paradise.

ALL CHILDREN: Yes, yes! Tell us about Paradise! Tell us!

(SHLEMAZL sits down and takes off his magic shoes.)

SHLEMAZL: Paradise? Paradise? *(holds up a shoe, peers at it, sighs)*

(LIGHTS OUT BRIEFLY, THEN UP AGAIN ON FAMILY AROUND TABLE. SOUND CUE: TUMLER plays violin, stops when lights come up; SHLEMAZL still holds a shoe, staring at it.)

TUMLER: And to this very day, Shlemazl gets up every morning. He eats his breakfast served by this woman who believes she's his wife, surrounded by these youngsters convinced they are his children . . .

(MRS. PLOSHER, KISHKE, BLINTZ, MAYOR FARMISHT and RABBI SHOFAR enter from left and stand around table.)

TUMLER: . . . amidst a whole village full of lunatics who think they've known him his entire life.

SHLEMAZL: *(to audience)* If I'd known Paradise was going to be so much like my old village, I wouldn't have maybe been in such a hurry to get there.

(LIGHTS OUT. SOUND CUE: TUMLER plays violin.)

THE END

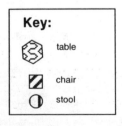

Stage Plan --*Shlemazl Goes to Paradise*

Key:
- table
- chair
- stool

THE MOST EXPENSIVE BONNET IN ALL INDIANA

In the early 1800s there were very few roads in North America, and most people traveled long distances either by rivers or by canals—waterways that connected one river to another. The boats that traveled the canals were called flatboats or barges and were pulled by teams of horses that walked on the river bank as the barge floated along the water in the canal. As a young man Abraham Lincoln worked on a flatboat, sailing from Illinois to New Orleans down the Ohio and Mississippi Rivers. Flatboat crews and captains took great pride in their vessels and often held races to see which boat was the fastest. *The Most Expensive Bonnet in All Indiana* is a tale about one such race, one of the last before the big steamboats and steam engine locomotives made flatboating obsolete as a major transportation method.

TIME: July 3–4, 1840

PLACE: Wabash & Erie Canal, Indiana

CAST:
Newsgirl Newspaper Reporter
Mr. Black Captain Lyon of the *Prairie Hen*
Mr. Brown *Prairie Hen* Navigator
Mrs. Snodgrass 8 Townspeople
Hail Columbia Navigator
Captain Snodgrass of the *Hail Columbia*
Jeremy Holcomb, *Prairie Hen* cabin boy

STAGE SET: a barrel; two stools; a boat frame

PROPS: checkers and checkerboard; newspapers; penny; parasol; coins; dollar bills; hatbox; cider flask; pocket watch; telescope; American flags; July 4th banners; red-white-and-blue bunting; handkerchief

SPECIAL EFFECTS: calliope or brass band music; fireworks sounds; *Yankee Doodle* played by a marching band

COSTUMES: mid-19th-century small-town dress for Newsgirl, Mr. Black, Mr. Brown, Townspeople, Newspaper Reporter; flatboat characters can wear nautical accessories—caps, bell-bottom trousers; navy jackets, etc.; Mrs. Snodgrass should have a fancy dress (hoop skirt) and a huge bonnet filled with beautiful flowers; her second bonnet should be just as huge but lopsided, filled with weeds, ridiculous

(LIGHTS UP on two men—MR. BROWN and MR. BLACK—playing checkers at stage right. A NEWSGIRL enters from stage left carrying newspapers and crosses to center stage.)

NEWSGIRL: Extra, extra, read all about it! The biggest flatboat race of the century starts today! Read all about it!

MR. BROWN: Say there, young lady; I'll take one of your newspapers.

(NEWSGIRL hands him a paper; MR. BROWN flips her a penny.)

NEWSGIRL: Gee, thanks, Mr. Brown! A brand new penny! *(exits right)*

MR. BROWN: 18 and 40. Can't get any newer than that.

MR. BLACK: *(wipes face with a kerchief)* Can't get any hotter, either, I'd say!

MR. BROWN: Well now, Mr. Black, it is the third of July in the heart of Indiana. It's supposed to be hotter than blue blazes! Do you think we'll see snow anytime soon?

MR. BLACK: We'll sooner see snow in July than the *Prairie Hen* win the race against *Hail Columbia*. What's that newspaper got to say about it?

MR. BROWN: Says the *Hail Columbia* is the fastest canal barge in the country. Captain Snodgrass predicts she'll make the trip down the Wabash & Erie Canal in record time.

MR. BLACK: That's no news! Every hightop skilletwhacker knows that.

MR. BROWN: Not the captain of the *Prairie Hen*. Why, this fellow Lyon says his little boat can get from Ft. Wayne to Wabash ahead of the *Hail Columbia* with hours to spare. And collect the five hundred dollar cash prize.

MR. BLACK: Pifflepoot and hogwash! Can't believe anything you read in a newspaper these days. Why, next thing you know, they'll be saying somebody's invented a steam engine that can roll along the ground on wheels!

MR. BROWN: *(jumps several of MR. BLACK'S checkers)* King me, Mr. Black!

(A crowd enters noisily from stage left. CAPTAIN SNODGRASS and MRS. SNODGRASS are in the lead followed by the HAIL COLUMBIA NAVIGATOR, a NEWSPAPER REPORTER and EIGHT TOWNSPEOPLE; all gather at center stage.)

CAPTAIN SNODGRASS: What a splendid day for a boat race! *Hail Columbia!*

TOWNSPEOPLE: *Hail Columbia!*

NEWSPAPER REPORTER: Captain Snodgrass, I'm a reporter with the *Ft. Wayne Sentinel.* How do you rate your chances in today's race?

CAPTAIN SNODGRASS: Welllll, I—

MRS. SNODGRASS: There's no question about it, young lady. The *Hail Columbia* is going to win the race in record time.

TOWNSPEOPLE: *Hail Columbia!*

NEWSPAPER REPORTER: Thank you, Mrs. Snodgrass. Now, Captain Snodgrass, the *Prairie Hen* is a smaller boat, but some say it's an improved model of barge with a modern keel design.

CAPTAIN SNODGRASS: Welllll, I—

MRS. SNODGRASS: Young lady, there is no better specimen of flatboat in existence today than the *Hail Columbia.* And you can quote Captain Snodgrass on that.

TOWNSPEOPLE: *Hail Columbia!*

NEWSPAPER REPORTER: Thank you, madam. One last question, Captain Snodgrass—

CAPTAIN SNODGRASS: Welllll, I—

MRS. SNODGRASS: *(prods the CAPTAIN with her parasol)* Oh, come along, Henry, you've talked enough already. It's time to start the race and win my five hundred dollars. *(to reporter)* I've ordered a new victory gown from St. Louis.

(CAPTAIN LYON, the PRAIRIE HEN NAVIGATOR and cabin boy JEREMY HOLCOMB enter from stage right; JEREMY stands shyly behind CAPTAIN LYON and the NAVIGATOR.)

NEWSPAPER REPORTER: There's Captain Lyon and the *Prairie Hen* crew!

TOWNSPEOPLE: *Prairie Hen! Prairie Hen!* The little boat with mighty men!

(CAPTAIN LYON crosses to center, shakes hands with CAPTAIN SNODGRASS, tips hat to MRS. SNODGRASS and addresses crowd.)

CAPTAIN LYON: Ladies and gentlemen, I'm proud to be here in Ft. Wayne this morning. I can't think of a better way to celebrate the

Fourth of July than by an old-fashioned test of skill and stamina. It shows the true American character—the competitive spirit that made this country what it is today!

TOWNSPEOPLE: What it is today!

CAPTAIN SNODGRASS: *(shakes LYON'S hand)* May the better boat win!

TOWNSPEOPLE: May the better boat win!

MRS. SNODGRASS: *(pulls husband away from LYON)* Don't worry, Henry. It already has.

(SOUND CUE: a blast of calliope music or brass band music, offstage.)

HAIL COLUMBIA NAVIGATOR: *(looks left)* By jiminy, here comes the circus wagon to see us off!

TOWNSPEOPLE: *Hail Columbia!* Mighty *Prairie Hen!*

(CAPTAIN LYON and PRAIRIE HEN NAVIGATOR exit right as JEREMY HOLCOMB lingers next to front of boat; TOWNSPEOPLE rush offstage left and MRS. SNODGRASS' bonnet is knocked to the ground and trampled.)

MRS. SNODGRASS: My bonnet! My special Fourth of July victory bonnet! Oh, it's ruined!

CAPTAIN SNODGRASS: Now, Zelda, don't get all bully-whanged! It's just a bonnet.

MRS. SNODGRASS: Just a bonnet? I was planning to wear it when we landed in Wabash. I can't make a public appearance without it. It wouldn't be proper. What would people think?

CAPTAIN SNODGRASS: They'd think you'd lost your marbles—er, your bonnet.

MRS. SNODGRASS: Henry Snodgrass!

CAPTAIN SNODGRASS: Now, you listen to me, Zelda: it's no use crying over spilt bonnets. You order a new one now and have it ready to pick up before we dock in Wabash. Now if you'll excuse me, I've got a race to run.

MRS. SNODGRASS: Very well, Henry.

(CAPTAIN SNODGRASS exits left; MRS. SNODGRASS turns and sees JEREMY, who is walking slowly right.)

MRS. SNODGRASS: Boy! I say there, boy!

JEREMY HOLCOMB: *(stops, turns)* Me, ma'am?

MRS. SNODGRASS: Do you see any other boys hereabouts?

JEREMY HOLCOMB: *(looks around)* No, ma'am.

MRS. SNODGRASS: Then run an errand for me. Take this hat to the milliner's shop and tell him I need another one just like it by tomorrow morning.

JEREMY HOLCOMB: Yes, ma'am. *(takes hat)*

MRS. SNODGRASS: Have him deliver it to Lagro, six miles north of Wabash. We'll be docking there tonight. And tell him to hurry, because we're in the middle of a boat race.

JEREMY HOLCOMB: Yes, ma'am. *(remains in place)*

MRS. SNODGRASS: Well? What are you waiting for?

JEREMY HOLCOMB: A tip, ma'am?

MRS. SNODGRASS: *(shakes her parasol at him)* Why, of all the cheek! Young ruffian!

(JEREMY scampers offstage right. SOUND CUE: a blast of calliope music or brass band music, offstage. MRS. SNODGRASS exits huffily offstage left, passing NEWSPAPER REPORTER who enters and stands down left; NEWSGIRL enters from right and stands down right next to MR. BLACK and MR. BROWN, who continue to play checkers.)

TOWNSPEOPLE: *(o.s.)* Hail Columbia! Mighty Prairie Hen!

NEWSPAPER REPORTER: The historic flatboat race between the *Hail Columbia* and *Prairie Hen* commenced at noon today, with the *Hail Columbia* opening a big lead.

NEWSGIRL: *Hail Columbia* opens big lead! Read all about it! *(passes papers to MR. BLACK and MR. BROWN)*

TOWNSPEOPLE: *(o.s.)* Hail Columbia! Mighty Prairie Hen!

NEWSPAPER REPORTER: As expected, Captain Snodgrass of the *Hail Columbia* had quite a bit to say—according to his wife. Said she, "I predict we'll win by a margin of two miles to one."

NEWSGIRL: *Hail Columbia* winning two miles to one! Read all about it! *(passes papers to MR. BLACK and MR. BROWN)*

TOWNSPEOPLE: *(o.s.)* Two miles to one! Two miles to one!

MR. BLACK: Two miles to one? Sounds like bunk to me!

MR. BROWN: Bunk to you?

MR. BLACK: Bunk to me! Why, it oughta be three!

NEWSPAPER REPORTER: And as twilight falls, the *Hail Columbia* docks in Lagro, still in the lead—

NEWSGIRL: *Hail Columbia* still in the lead! *(passes papers to MR. BLACK and MR. BROWN)*

TOWNSPEOPLE: *(o.s.)* Still in the lead! Still in the lead!

MR. BROWN: I'll wager the *Prairie Hen* gets there first!

MR. BLACK: Gets there first? Why you're crazy as a loon!

TOWNSPEOPLE: *(o.s.)* Crazy as a loon!

MR. BROWN: *(lays a stack of coins on barrel)* I'll let my money call the tune!

MR. BLACK: *(lays a stack of dollar bills on top of coins)* I'll match your tune and call my own!

MR. BROWN: And who pays the piper—

MR. BLACK: We'll see right soon.

TOWNSPEOPLE: *(o.s.)* See right soon! Crazy as a loon!

> *(SOUND CUE: a blast of calliope music or brass band music, offstage. NEWSPAPER REPORTER exits left, NEWSGIRL exits right, MR. BROWN and MR. BLACK exit right. HAIL COLUMBIA NAVIGATOR and CAPTAIN SNODGRASS enter from behind the boat.)*

HAIL COLUMBIA NAVIGATOR: There she lays, Captain. All steady astern and ready to go ashore.

CAPTAIN SNODGRASS: Good work, crew! We're just six miles from the finish line. You can rest a bit.

HAIL COLUMBIA NAVIGATOR: When do we shove off?

CAPTAIN SNODGRASS: Just long enough to pick up a parcel. Has anyone seen the *Prairie Hen*?

HAIL COLUMBIA NAVIGATOR: Not since we rounded the bend back there at Maumee Ferry. Why, that was hours ago!

CAPTAIN SNODGRASS: Good. When I return, we can pull anchor and be in Wabash by midnight.

HAIL COLUMBIA NAVIGATOR: Aye-aye, captain.

> *(NAVIGATOR exits left; MRS. SNODGRASS enters from behind boat.)*

MRS. SNODGRASS: Henry!

CAPTAIN SNODGRASS: Yes, dear?

MRS. SNODGRASS: Henry, I've been thinking.

CAPTAIN SNODGRASS: Oh no. I mean—yes, dear?

MRS. SNODGRASS: It doesn't make a lick of sense to arrive in Wabash in the middle of the night. Why, who's going to be there to greet us? Will the marching band be there? Will the mayor and city council be there? Will the fine gentlemen and leading ladies of the town be there with the fireworks and parade?

CAPTAIN SNODGRASS: Yes, dear. I mean, no, dear. I mean—

MRS. SNODGRASS: Henry, if we dock in Wabash surrounded by nothing but pitch dark and hoot owls, no one will see my new bonnet. And that's just not fair. *(takes out handkerchief, begins sobbing)*

CAPTAIN SNODGRASS: Yes, dear. I mean, no, dear. I mean—

MRS. SNODGRASS: The least you can do is wait until daylight when we can make a proper entrance. *(sobs)* And be properly appreciated.

CAPTAIN SNODGRASS: Very well. Navigator, tell the crew we'll pull anchor at four a.m. That will get us to Wabash by dawn.

MRS. SNODGRASS: Thank you, Henry. Now, where is my new bonnet?

CAPTAIN SNODGRASS: I was just going to see about that, my dear. You go back to sleep and get your beauty rest.

(MRS. SNODGRASS exits left; CAPTAIN SNODGRASS goes to center stage and gazes around anxiously.)

CAPTAIN SNODGRASS: Well, this is a fine howdy-you-do! That milliner was supposed to be here at the dock with the new bonnet. Mrs. Snodgrass is going to be most distressed.

(JEREMY HOLCOMB walks slowly onstage from right; he has a black mustache and carries a hatbox.)

JEREMY HOLCOMB: Captain Snodgrass?

CAPTAIN SNODGRASS: Aye! Are you the milliner?

JEREMY HOLCOMB: Nosir, I'm the milliner's apprentice. The milliner has met with an unfortunate accident.

CAPTAIN SNODGRASS: Accident?

JEREMY HOLCOMB: Yessir, he fell off his horse.

CAPTAIN SNODGRASS: That's terrible!

JEREMY HOLCOMB: There's worse, sir.

CAPTAIN SNODGRASS: Worse?

JEREMY HOLCOMB: He fell on top of the new bonnet he had just made. The bonnet for Mrs. Snodgrass. It was completely destroyed.

CAPTAIN SNODGRASS: Great squonk! That's a disaster! What am I going to do? Can you help? You're an apprentice. Can you make a bonnet?

JEREMY HOLCOMB: Well, sir, I can surely try. *(wobbles)* Oh my, I've got to sit down.

CAPTAIN SNODGRASS: *(helps him to a stool)* There you go. You look mighty tuckered out, son.

JEREMY HOLCOMB: Yessir, I've ridden horseback all the way from Ft. Wayne.

CAPTAIN SNODGRASS: Ft. Wayne! Why, that is a long day's ride. You should have been with me on board the *Hail Columbia.* Smooth and easy, just floating down the water without a care in the world.

JEREMY HOLCOMB: Well, sir, I got here as fast as I could. Why, I even passed that other boat along the way.

CAPTAIN SNODGRASS: Other boat? Oh, you mean the *Prairie Hen!* Haw-haw-haw! You could have passed that walking! Haw-haw-haw! Could have passed it crawling! Haw-haw-haw!

JEREMY HOLCOMB: *(to audience)* Is he in for a surprise!

CAPTAIN SNODGRASS: All right, then, son, snap to and spin me a bonnet! I can't leave town without it.

JEREMY HOLCOMB: Yes, sir! *(opens the hatbox and looks inside)* Now, you understand, sir, we don't usually do a rush order like this. My master is awfully proud of his reputation as a craftsman. He hates to turn out anything that doesn't do him or the customer justice.

CAPTAIN SNODGRASS: *(pulls out several dollar bills and stuffs them in Jeremy's hand)* Of course, of course. Justice, yes, indeed. Take these and see if they'll speed up the creative process. There'll be plenty more where those came from soon enough.

JEREMY HOLCOMB: I believe there will be, sir. Say, are you thirsty?

CAPTAIN SNODGRASS: Thirsty? Why, I believe I am.

JEREMY HOLCOMB: *(takes a wine flask from his coat)* I've got some hard cider here. Fresh-squeezed.

CAPTAIN SNODGRASS: *(takes flask from JEREMY)* Fresh-squeezed, you say? Well, just a little sip wouldn't do any harm. Mmmm, don't need to tell my wife.

JEREMY HOLCOMB: Nosir. Wouldn't dream of it.

CAPTAIN SNODGRASS: *(drinks)* Ahhhhh! Delicious! *(pulls up the other stool, sits)* Guess I'll just settle back here and wait. *(drinks two or three times, nods)* Yessssss, I'll just settle…back…*(falls asleep)*

(SOUND CUE: a blast of calliope music or brass band music, offstage. JEREMY peels off his mustache and exits right. NEWSPAPER REPORTER enters left, NEWSGIRL enters right. PRAIRIE HEN NAVIGATOR and CAPTAIN LYON enter from behind the boat; NAVIGATOR turns wheel, CAPTAIN LYON peers ahead with telescope.)

NEWSPAPER REPORTER: Well, all through the night, the little *Prairie Hen* kept moving and hauling—

TOWNSPEOPLE: *(o.s.)* Moving and hauling! Moving and hauling!

NEWSGIRL: *Prairie Hen* gains while *Hail Columbia* sleeps! Read all about it!

TOWNSPEOPLE: *(o.s.)* *Prairie Hen* gains! Read all about it!

NEWSGIRL: *(nudges sleeping CAPTAIN SNODGRASS)* Read all about it! Read all about it!

(CAPTAIN SNODGRASS awakes, looks at watch, jumps up and starts to runs offstage left, forgetting hat box.)

MRS. SNODGRASS: *(o.s.)* Henry!

(CAPTAIN SNODGRASS stops, realizes he's left the hat box, then runs back and retrieves it before dashing offstage left.)

PRAIRIE HEN NAVIGATOR: Captain Lyon! Look up ahead!

CAPTAIN LYON: Great jumping jillywads! It's Wabash! It's the finish line!

PRAIRIE HEN NAVIGATOR: We've won! We've won! We've beaten the *Hail Columbia!*

(CAPTAIN and NAVIGATOR slap each other on shoulders.)

CAPTAIN LYON: I can't believe my own eyes! We've beaten the fastest flatboat on the canal! And, look, there's young Jeremy Holcomb waiting at the dock! I thought he was on board with us! (*looks through telescope*) What's he doing with that…that…that hat box in his hands?

(*SOUND CUE: Yankee Doodle played by marching band, fade under at dialogue. TOWNSPEOPLE enter cheering from left and converge around CAPTAIN LYON and the PRAIRIE HEN NAVIGATOR; MR. BROWN and MR. BLACK enter from right and sit on stools, resuming their checker game after MR. BLACK pays MR. BROWN his bet; JEREMY HOLCOMB enters from right and stands with CAPTAIN LYON. TOWNSPEOPLE carry American flags and July 4th banners; they trim the boat in red-white-and-blue bunting.*)

NEWSGIRL: (*hands papers to MR. BLACK and MR. BROWN*) Extra! Extra! The *Prairie Hen* beats *Hail Columbia* by fifteen minutes! It's a new canal record!

TOWNSPEOPLE: Hurrah for the *Prairie Hen!* Hurrah! Hurrah!

(*TOWNSPEOPLE shake hands of Prairie Hen crew as CAPTAIN SNODGRASS rushes onstage from left, followed by HAIL COLUMBIA NAVIGATOR and MRS. SNODGRASS carrying her new bonnet.*)

CAPTAIN SNODGRASS: (to *Hail Columbia* Navigator) This is impossible! Beaten by that floating tea cup! How in the world could this have happened?

JEREMY HOLCOMB: It's a known fact that hard cider makes one early to bed and late to rise.

CAPTAIN SNODGRASS: (*stares wildly around*) Who said that?

MRS. SNODGRASS: Henry, I don't like this new bonnet! It's simply not the quality to which I am accustomed. It looks like it was made by a child! Take it back. I won't wear it!

(*She hands the bonnet to CAPTAIN SNODGRASS; he looks at it, gets ready to throw it into the audience, then places it securely on her head.*)

CAPTAIN SNODGRASS: You'll wear it and you'll like it! Getting this dadblamed bonnet cost me the race—and five hundred dollars!

MRS. SNODGRASS: But, Henry, this has got to be the ugliest bonnet in all Indiana!

CAPTAIN SNODGRASS: That may be true, Zelda, but at five hundred dollars, it is also the most expensive bonnet in all Indiana!

NEWSGIRL: Extra! Extra! Read all about it! The most expensive bonnet in all Indiana!

(*SOUND CUE:* Yankee Doodle *played by marching band. Everyone sings to tune of* Yankee Doodle:)

EVERYONE: *(sings)*
verse:
    Yankee Doodle rode upon
    A flatboat oh so merry
    A cabin boy, he won the day
    With a bonnet quite contrary
chorus:
    Prairie Hen, she won the race
    Her fame is known all over
    Hail Columbia, all she got
    Was a bonnet full of clover

(*MUSIC STOPS.*)

EVERYONE: *(cheers)* Hurrah, *Prairie Hen!* Hurrah, *Hail Columbia!* Hurrah, United States of America!

(*LIGHTS OUT.*)

THE END

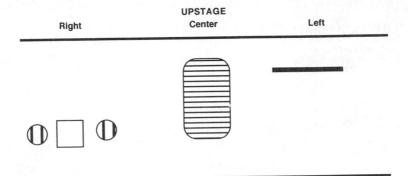

Stage Plan *The Most Expensive Bonnet in All Indiana*

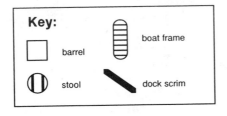

Key:

☐ barrel

🎛 boat frame

◉ stool

◥ dock scrim

RETURN OF THE RED PHANTOM

Return of the Red Phantom is drawn from sea lore of the American clipper ship period, an era of nautical history that extended from the 1830s to the 1860s. The clipper ships were specially constructed to be the fastest oceangoing vessels of the day; the name "clipper" came from their ability to "clip," or shorten, sailing time from a standard passage. In 1851 the clipper ship *Flying Cloud* sailed from New York City to San Francisco (all the way around the bottom tip of South America) in what was then a world's record 89 days—even after losing her main and mizzen top-gallant masts in a storm. At first the clipper ships were hired primarily to carry cargo; when gold was discovered in California in 1848, however, they took on increasing numbers of gold-seekers looking for the quickest way to get from the Atlantic Coast to the Pacific Coast.

TIME: Late last night

PLACE: Cape Sebastian, southern Oregon

CAST: Grandpa (or Grandma)   First Mate Hatch
          Billy   Bosun Eldridge
          Beverly   Cook Barlow
          Captain Silas Collins   6 Crew Members (male or female)
          Ansel Collins

STAGE SET: chair; two stools

PROPS: book; bag of food; a knife; a pistol; a sword

COSTUMES: Grandpa, Billy and Beverly dress contemporary casual; others wear mid-19th-century seafaring garb, as in *Moby Dick*

(LIGHTS UP FULL; at stage right GRANDPA sits in a chair, reading a book. Two children, BILLY and BEVERLY, enter from left, skipping to where he sits. They stop and face him.)

BILLY & BEVERLY: Hi, Grandpa!

GRANDPA: Hello, Billy and Beverly. How are you this fine evening?

BILLY & BEVERLY: Grandpa, we're bored!

GRANDPA: Bored? How can you be bored? Summer vacation has just started. Why, it's only the middle of June.

BILLY: Grandpa, it's not like we don't enjoy visiting you out here in the country . . .

BEVERLY: But, can we go to town and rent a video tonight?

BILLY: Something really exciting!

BEVERLY: With a lot of action!

GRANDPA: *(chuckles)* So it's action and excitement you want, eh? Well, keep your lids on, youngsters. You're liable to get plenty before the night's out.

BEVERLY: What do you mean, Grandpa? What's going to happen tonight? Here?

BILLY: Maybe a big party of wild pirates will walk in the door!

GRANDPA: Actually, Billy, you're not far wrong. After all, it is Sailorman's Eve. And that usually means quite a bit of action here on the Pacific Coast of Oregon.

BILLY: Sailorman's Eve? What's that?

GRANDPA: Today is June the twenty-first, the day before summer, or Midsummer Eve. In seafaring towns like this one it's known as Sailorman's Eve—the night when all the ships and sailors that have been lost at sea are said to return home for a few hours before the break of dawn.

BEVERLY: Awww, Grandpa, that's silly! You're talking about, like, ghosts, or something? Nobody believes that stuff!

GRANDPA: If you look out the window, you can see Cape Sebastian from here. That's where they pass, all in a long line.

(BILLY walks a few paces to stage left and looks into the distance.)

GRANDPA: The *Brutus*. The *Ulysses*. The *Sparrowhawk*. The *Halifax*. Whalers, packets, moonrakers and schooners, all rising from the salty mist and coursing through the rippling tide.

BILLY: I don't know, Grandpa. Who would want to come back to an out-of-the-way little town like this? If I sailed away on a ship, I'd never come back.

GRANDPA: Captain Silas Collins and his son, Ansel, might.

BEVERLY: Who are they?

GRANDPA: Silas Collins was one of the finest captains ever sailed a clipper ship. Back in the 1840s he could run a four-master from Provincetown to San Diego all the way around Cape Horn in three months. In the days before steamships, that was a world record.

BILLY: *(looks to left)* Hey! There's a light out there!

BEVERLY: *(runs up next to him and peers out "the window")* Where? Where?

GRANDPA: The year 1848 found Silas Collins piloting a proud, tall clipper from Valparaiso to Seattle—the *Red Phantom*, she was called. His twelve-year-old son, Ansel, served as cabin boy, and they made good time until putting into San Francisco.

BEVERLY: I see it!

BILLY: *(points)* And there's another one over there! And over there!

GRANDPA: As you might remember, 1848 was the year gold was discovered in California. Gold Rush fever had captured the entire country. Why, people were coming to California from as far as England and even China to see if they could strike it rich. Silas took on fresh supplies at San Francisco and could barely keep his crew from running off to the gold fields.

BEVERLY: Grandpa…what are all those lights in the water?

BILLY: They're moving…they're…now they've gone away.

GRANDPA: Well, the *Red Phantom* headed north and wasn't two days out of port when the first mate and bosun stirred up the crew. It was mutiny on the high seas, and though Silas Collins tried his best to stop them, the greedy rebels seized the ship and turned back to San Francisco.

BEVERLY: That's terrible! What did they to do to Captain Collins and Ansel?

GRANDPA: The mutineers put them overboard on a small rowing skiff with four days' food and water. They were never heard from again.

BILLY: And the *Red Phantom*?

GRANDPA: On the way south, the *Red Phantom* hit a shoal just past Point Reyes—and went down with all hands.

BEVERLY: Gee, Grandpa, that's pretty creepy. I'm glad I don't believe in ghosts or—

(SOUND CUE: a sound of singing offstage, distant, then louder, the sea shanty Congo River. *BILLY and BEVERLY stare toward left; GRANDPA returns to reading his book.)*

VOICES: *(o.s., sing)*
Have you ever been on the Congo River?
Blow, boys, blow
Where the fever makes you moan and shiver?
Blow, you bonny boys, blow

BILLY: It sounds like somebody singing.

(Singing stops. SOUND CUE: a loud, slow door knocking; knocking stops.)

BEVERLY: Grandpa, somebody's at the door.

GRANDPA: You're right about that, young lady.

(For several seconds no one moves or speaks; BILLY and BEVERLY continue to stare toward left; the knocking comes again, then stops.)

BILLY: Shouldn't somebody answer?

GRANDPA: Oh, they'll let themselves in. The way they do every year.

(BILLY and BEVERLY back up toward GRANDPA, who continues to read. SOUND CUE: a door creaks open. A MAN [CAPTAIN SILAS COLLINS] and A BOY [ANSEL COLLINS] dressed in 19th-century sailor outfits enter from left; they walk slowly to center stage, as if confused.)

CAPTAIN COLLINS: Hallo! Margaret? Margaret, are you at home?

ANSEL COLLINS: Father, why is there no one in our house? Where have mother and sister gone?

CAPTAIN COLLINS: I do not know, Ansel. We have been away at sea a long time. Hallo! Hallo! Has anyone seen Margaret Collins and her baby? Hallo! The house is deserted. I fear they have departed.

ANSEL COLLINS: I hope we find them soon.

BILLY: *(speaks to CAPTAIN COLLINS and ANSEL but gets no response)* Hey! Hey, you!

BEVERLY: Be careful, Billy!

GRANDPA: Don't worry. They can't hear us. Can't see us, either. In their eyes, this house looks just the way it did when they last saw it…more then a hundred and fifty years ago.

ANSEL COLLINS: What shall we do, father?

CAPTAIN COLLINS: A chill breeze blows off the Cape. Let us warm ourselves at the fire and wait awhile.

(CAPTAIN COLLINS and ANSEL pull up stools and sit at down center, facing audience, spreading hands as if warming themselves at a fireplace. SOUND CUE: thumping and shouting offstage left.)

CREW MEMBER #1: *(o.s.)* They've gone below. Now's the time to get 'em, I say!

CREW MEMBER #2: *(o.s.)* He's right! Time's a-wasting! Come on!

(SIX CREW MEMBERS led by FIRST MATE HATCH and BOSUN ELDRIDGE burst onstage from left with COOK BARLOW bringing up the rear. The CREW MEMBERS rush over to CAPTAIN COLLINS and SILAS, grab them from their stools and present them at center stage to HATCH and ELDRIDGE.)

CAPTAIN COLLINS: Hatch, Eldridge, all you men. Stand down, I order you.

HATCH: You're not giving anymore orders on this ship, Captain. I am.

SIX CREW MEMBERS: Yezzah! Yezzah!

HATCH: And hereafter, you may address me as Captain Hatch. Ex-first mate, now captain of the *Red Phantom.*

CAPTAIN COLLINS: This is mutiny!

ELDRIDGE: We know what it is. And we know you can't do nothing about it.

CAPTAIN COLLINS: Men, be reasonable. Has your lust for gold obliterated your common sense? We cannot turn back now. There is a southwester coming up strong. If we keep our course, we can stay ahead of it. If not, we shall run straight into the teeth of a gale that will rip this vessel to planking.

CREW MEMBER #3: He'll talk till he's blue in the face. I say we hang 'im from the yardarm right this very minute. Him and his blodgy cabin boy.

HATCH: Hold steady, sailor. I'm in charge here. And I say there'll be no hanging without a fair trial.

SIX CREW MEMBERS: Yezzah! Yezzah!

(CREW MEMBERS sit CAPTAIN COLLINS and ANSEL on stools facing stage left, then stand behind them upstage; HATCH and ELDRIDGE stand together facing CAPTAIN COLLINS and ANSEL; COOK BARLOW stands behind them.)

HATCH: Bosun Eldridge, cite the charges against the accused.

ELDRIDGE: Firstwith, upon the night of June the seventh, eighteen and forty-eight, Captain Silas Collins—the accused—did maliciously refuse First Mate Hatch's request to break out extra rations of rum for the crew.

CAPTAIN COLLINS: This is a commercial cargo ship not a grog-soaked pleasure skivvy! I will not command a lot of drunken—

HATCH: The prisoner will be silent!

ELDRIDGE: Charge the second: upon the afternoon of June the eleventh, Captain Silas Collins did command Crewman Carson to be unlawfully restrained and confined to his bunk below deck.

CREW MEMBER #4: He did so, he did! I was bound and trussed like a pig on the table at Christmas dinner, I was! Stuck down in that black hole without so much as a whiff of fresh salt air!

CAPTAIN COLLINS: Carson had attempted, against my explicit order, to take unauthorized liberty and jump ship. His hands were tied to prevent him from assaulting the cabin boy who reported his transgression.

ELDRIDGE: Charge the third: upon the afternoon of June the seventeenth, the aforementioned Captain was overheard ordering said cabin boy to rummage through the store bag of Crewman O'Farrell—for the purpopse of illegally removing private property.

ANSEL COLLINS: *(jumps up)* That's a bald-faced lie! O'Farrell is a dirty, rotten—

HATCH: Bosun, secure the prisoner!

(ELDRIDGE and CREW MEMBERS #5 and #6 grab ANSEL and set him down on stool.)

CREWMAN #5 (O'FARRELL): Caught him red-handed, I did, with his rancid mitts inside my swagpouch.

CAPTAIN COLLINS: My son is no thief. Nor am I. However, I possessed reliable information indicating that Crewman O'Farrell had stolen certain navigational charts for the purpose, I believe, of misleading the vessel from its assigned course.

HATCH: And where did you get that so-called reliable information?

CAPTAIN COLLINS: I will not answer that question.

HATCH: You're on trial—trial for your life. You will answer all questions put to you by this tribunal.

CAPTAIN COLLINS: You have no authority—

HATCH: I have command of the crew and this ship. That is my authority. I call Cook Barlow to the witness stand.

(COOK BARLOW steps forward hesitantly.)

HATCH: Do you swear to tell the truth, the whole truth and nothing but the truth, so help you God?

COOK BARLOW: I-I-I do.

HATCH: It was you who told Silas Collins about the alleged theft of charts?

COOK BARLOW: Well, I-I-I…yes, I suppose I did.

CREW MEMBER #6: Bleedin' informer!

ELDRIDGE: Silence in the court!

HATCH: And what did you tell the Captain?

COOK BARLOW: I-I-I…well, the Captain asked me if I had any idea of where the missing charts might be. And I-I-I-I told him I had heard somebody—wasn't sure who 'cause I didn't rightly see 'em as they were talking—tell somebody else that the charts had been filched by a crew member.

ANSEL COLLINS: That's a lie! He came to my father and said O'Farrell had stolen the charts.

ELDRIDGE: Silence!

ANSEL COLLINS: And said he'd stand watch while I went and got them back!

HATCH: One more word from you, my lad, and I'll put you in irons. Silas Collins, what have you to say to this man's testimony?

(Captain Collins stands slowly and faces Cook Barlow, who refuses to look at him.)

CAPTAIN COLLINS: I am truly ashamed. Ashamed for you, Cook Barlow. Ashamed for the lies and the perjury you have uttered. Ashamed for the trust and the friendship you have betrayed. You have served with me as a loyal crewman for more than twenty years. Now you repay my generosity and trust with perfidy and cowardice.

CREW MEMBER #1: Enough speeches! Let the jury vote!

CREW MEMBER #2: Aye, let the jury vote! Guilty as charged, say I!

CREW MEMBER #3: Guilty!

CREW MEMBER #4: Guilty!

CREW MEMBER #5: Guilty!

CREW MEMBER #6: Guilty!

CREW MEMBER #1: Guilty on all counts!

ELDRIDGE: The prisoners will stand to receive sentence!

(CAPTAIN COLLINS and ANSEL stand.)

HATCH: Silas and Ansel Collins, you've heard the verdict. It is now time for me, as commanding officer, to pass sentence upon your crimes.

COOK BARLOW: *(kneels before Hatch)* Please, don't kill them. They was only doin' their duty. And young Ansel…he's only a boy.

ELDRIDGE: Get up, you weasel! Or you're liable to suffer the same!

(BARLOW rises slowly and retreats behind HATCH.)

HATCH: As punishment befitting their crimes, at six bells the prisoners will be lowered into a shallop and set adrift with two days' rations.

COOK BARLOW: Two days! They'll never make shore in two days! Have mercy! They can have my share of grub for the next two weeks!

HATCH: Very well. I shall be merciful. Four days' rations. If you're the brilliant pilot you're cracked up to be, Collins, you'll have no trouble reaching land by then. Away then!

CREW MEMBERS: Away! Away!

(COOK BARLOW hands ANSEL a bag of food and hugs him. Crew members turn ANSEL and CAPTAIN COLLINS around twice, then sit them down on stools facing audience. CREW MEMBERS, HATCH and ELDRIDGE exit left, laughing and singing Congo River; *BARLOW exits last, turns and gives a sad wave.)*

CREW: *(sing)*
   A Yankee ship came down the river
   Blow, boys, blow!
   Her masts and spars they shone like silver
   Blow, you bonny boys, blow!

   (CAPTAIN COLLINS and ANSEL make slow rowing motions and do not speak for several seconds.)

ANSEL COLLINS: Father, are you frightened?
CAPTAIN COLLINS: Frightened? Of the sea? *(chuckles)* No, son. Men like us cannot be frightened of the sea. She is our angel, our helpmate and taskmaster. She is the source of our life's noble work and our life's humble pleasures. She is our destiny, and whatever fate this life brings us serves her inscrutable purpose.

   (They row silently for another few seconds.)

ANSEL COLLINS: Father, will we ever see mother and sister again?
CAPTAIN COLLINS: We shall not cease traveling until we do. That I promise you, my son. We shall find them, though we search through the rest of eternity.

   (They row silently for another few seconds, then stop and rise and walk slowly left, exiting. SOUND CUE: a door creaks open, then shuts.)

BILLY: That couldn't have been real. We must have been out in the sun too long today.
GRANDPA: Happens every Midsummer Eve. Just the way you saw it.

   (BEVERLY crosses to center stage where CREW MEMBERS had been standing, waves her arms around as if trying to touch something.)

BEVERLY: It was like they were right in this room. A moment from the past walked right into this room. And we all saw it!
GRANDPA: We all saw the sun rise today, didn't we? We all see that wall, those candles, this book.

   (BILLY takes book from GRANDPA'S hand and holds it up.)

BILLY: But those things are real! We see them because they're here! Every day! We can touch them!

GRANDPA: And just because something isn't here every day makes it less real? Or because you can't touch it? Or think you can't, maybe.

BEVERLY: Grandpa, I feel so sad for the Captain and his boy. They just keep wandering around, looking for their family. It's like a nightmare that never stops. Isn't there anything we can do?

GRANDPA: Everything we experience in our world can't always be perfectly explained. Right now, we don't understand why Captain Collins and Ansel come back to Cape Sebastian every Sailorman's Eve. It's a secret the universe isn't willing to share with us just yet. Then again, maybe you two will grow up and find the answer.

BILLY: We could be scientists!

BEVERLY: We could discover another dimension!

GRANDPA: You could also get ready for bed. It's about that time…in this dimension, anyway. *(yawns and stretches, stands)* Goodnight, kids. See you tomorrow. *(exits right)*

BILLY & BEVERLY: Goodnight, Grandpa.

(BILLY and Beverly move to center stage and stare out "window.")

BILLY: Wow, the evening really went by fast.

BEVERLY: Want to watch television?

BILLY: Nah. I'm going to watch the ocean for awhile.

BEVERLY: It's a clear night. Quiet, too.

(BILLY hums Congo River.*)*

BEVERLY: What's that?

BILLY: Oh, nothing. Just a tune I heard somewhere.

(SOUND CUE: a sound of singing offstage, distant, then louder [Congo River]; BILLY and BEVERLY join in on third line.)

VOICES: *(o.s.)*
Blow you winds and blow forever
Blow, boys, blow!
Blow me down the Congo River
Blow, you bonny boys, blow!

(LIGHTS OUT.)

THE END

Congo River

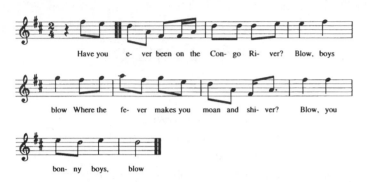

Have you e- ver been on the Con- go Ri- ver? Blow, boys

blow Where the fe- ver makes you moan and shi- ver? Blow, you

bon- ny boys, blow

*** UPSTAGE *·

Right   Center   Left

Stage Plan --*The Return of the Red Phantom*

Key:

▪ chair

⊘ stool

The Author

L.E. McCULLOUGH, PH.D. is a playwright, composer and ethnomusicologist whose studies in music and folklore have spanned cultures throughout the world. Formerly Assistant Director of the Indiana University School of Music at Indianapolis and a touring artist with Young Audiences, Inc., Dr. McCullough has performed for elementary and high schools throughout the U.S. and has recorded with Irish, French, Cajun, Latin, blues, jazz, country, bluegrass and rock ensembles on 31 albums for Angel/EMI, Log Cabin, Kicking Mule, Rounder, Bluezette and other independent labels. Winner of the 1995 Playwrights' Preview Productions Emerging Playwright Award, his Celtic Ballet, *Connlaoi's Tale: The Woman Who Danced On Waves,* received its world premiere with Dance Kaleidoscope in March, 1995; his book of original stage monologues, *Ice Babies in Oz,* was published in April, 1995, by Smith & Kraus, Inc.; his stage play, *Blues for Miss Buttercup,* debuted in New York in June, 1995. He is the author of *The Complete Irish Tinwhistle Tutor* and *Favorite Irish Session Tunes,* two highly acclaimed music instruction books, and has composed filmscores for three PBS specials—*Alone Together, A Place Just Right* and *John Kane.* Since 1991 Dr. McCullough has received 35 awards in 26 national literary competitions and had 178 poem and short story publications in 90 North American literary journals. Dr. McCullough is a member of The Dramatists Guild, Inc. and the American Conference for Irish Studies.